Low-Carb Diet Cookbook For Beginners

Nourish Your Body, Elevate Your Lifestyle.
Low-Carb Eating Made Easy.
Delicious & Simple Recipes for Vibrant Living.

D1519093

Scarlet May Lee

TABLE OF CONTENTS

Chapter 1. Introduction

Welcome to the world of delicious and nutritious low-carb eating!

Life can be extremely stressful, leaving little time and energy for healthy meal planning and preparation.
Consider these scenarios: a busy professional must balance work, personal commitments, and keeping a healthy lifestyle. Similarly, a health-conscious newbie may be just getting started on her/his path to a more healthy lifestyle. A fitness enthusiast, on the other hand, is constantly looking for ways to improve performance and attain his/her fitness goals. And last but not least, a wellness seeker, is looking to kickstart a health-conscious way of life.

Each of these folks has their own problems, desires, needs, and frustrations, and they wish to approach the low-carb diet for a variety of reasons, but they all ultimately want the same thing: a higher quality of life. They want to be happy!

This is where this book comes into play. We understand your individual requirements, desires, pain areas, and frustrations, and we designed this guide with **You** in mind. We will provide you with the foundation and confidence to navigate the world of low-carb eating successfully.

With our comprehensive guide, you'll discover the simplicity and power of a low-carb diet. This cookbook, written specifically for you, provides practical ideas, simple recipes, and knowledge insights to help you reach your health and weight loss goals. Say goodbye to time-consuming meal preparation and welcome to tasty, wholesome meals that will fuel your body and mind. Whether you're looking for convenience or starting a new health adventure, this will become your go-to reference for adopting the low-carb lifestyle and improving your state of wellness.

The Power of a Low-Carb Diet

A low-carb diet is not just another passing fad: it is a scientifically backed approach to healthy eating that has gained immense popularity in recent years. By reducing your carbohydrate intake and focusing on whole, unprocessed foods, you can unlock a multitude of benefits for your body and mind.

Numerous studies have shown that low-carb diets can be highly effective for weight loss and weight management. When you limit your intake of carbohydrates, your body turns to stored fat as its primary fuel source. This metabolic shift leads to a state called *Ketosis*, where your body produces ketones that provide energy and support fat burning. By following a low-carb diet, you can experience sustainable weight loss while preserving lean muscle mass.

Beyond weight loss, a low-carb diet can also have positive impacts on various health markers. It has been shown to improve blood sugar control, insulin sensitivity, and reduce the risk of developing type 2 diabetes. Low-carb eating can also lead to lower triglyceride levels, increased levels of HDL (good) cholesterol, and improved blood pressure, all of which contribute to better cardiovascular health.

Furthermore, many individuals report increased mental clarity, improved energy levels, and reduced cravings when following a low-carb diet. By stabilizing blood sugar levels and avoiding the rollercoaster ride of energy crashes associated with high-carb meals, you can experience sustained energy throughout the day and improved cognitive function.

The Foundation of Low-Carb Eating

At its core, a low-carb diet involves reducing your intake of carbohydrates and replacing them with healthy fats, lean proteins, and plenty of non-starchy vegetables. By focusing on nutrient-dense, whole foods, you provide your body with the building blocks it needs for optimal health and vitality.

Carbohydrates come in various forms, including simple sugars found in sweets, fruits, and processed foods, as well as complex carbohydrates found in grains, legumes, and starchy vegetables. While carbohydrates can be an important source of energy, excessive consumption, especially of refined carbohydrates, can lead to weight gain and other health issues.

By reducing your carbohydrate intake and selecting high-quality sources of carbohydrates, such as non-starchy vegetables and small amounts of fruits, you can achieve a balanced and sustainable low-carb diet. This approach allows you to enjoy a wide variety of flavors and textures while keeping your blood sugar levels stable and supporting your health goals.

Navigating the Low-Carb Journey

As you embark on your low-carb journey, it's important to approach it with a mindset of exploration and learning. This book will serve as your guide, providing you with the tools and knowledge necessary to navigate this lifestyle successfully. We will cover a wide range of topics, including meal planning, recipe ideas, tips for dining out, and strategies to overcome challenges along the way.

Throughout this book, you will find evidence-based information supported by scientific research. It's essential to rely on reputable sources when making dietary changes, and we have incorporated scientific references to back up the information provided. We encourage you to explore these references and delve deeper into the science behind low-carb eating.

Additionally, we will include practical tips and suggestions to help you overcome common challenges and frustrations. We understand that change can be daunting, but with the right mindset and guidance, you can create a sustainable lifestyle that suits your needs and preferences.

So, whether you're a busy professional seeking convenient meal options or a health-conscious novice eager to embark on a healthier path, this book is here to support you. We will provide you with the inspiration, knowledge, and delicious recipes you need to make low-carb eating a seamless part of your life.

Get ready to start a journey of nourishment and transformation. Let's dive into the world of low-carb eating and discover the countless benefits it can bring to your health and well-being. Together, we will make healthy eating simple, enjoyable, and sustainable.

Note: Before beginning any weight-loss plan, consult with your doctor, especially if you have a medical condition such as diabetes or heart disease.

To explore this topic further:

[1] https://www.mayoclinic.org/healthy-lifestyle/weight-loss/in-depth/low-carb-diet/art-20045831
[2] https://pubmed.ncbi.nlm.nih.gov/19082851/
[3] https://www.hsph.harvard.edu/nutritionsource/carbohydrates/low-carbohydrate-diets/

Chapter 2. Understanding the Low-Carb Diet

In this chapter, we will delve into the fundamentals of a low-carb diet, exploring its principles, benefits, and the science behind its effectiveness. By gaining a deeper understanding of the low-

carb approach, you will be empowered to make informed choices and embrace this lifestyle with confidence.

What is a Low-Carb Diet?

A low-carb diet involves reducing your intake of carbohydrates while increasing your consumption of healthy fats and proteins. By minimizing your reliance on carbs, you shift your body's primary fuel source from glucose to fat, leading to a state of ketosis.

Carbohydrates are the body's main source of energy, found in foods like grains, fruits, starchy vegetables, and sugars. However, consuming excessive carbohydrates can lead to spikes in blood sugar levels, insulin resistance, and weight gain. By reducing your carb intake, you can encourage your body to utilize stored fat as its primary source of fuel, resulting in weight loss and numerous other health benefits.

The Benefits of a Low-Carb Diet

The benefits of a low-carb diet extend far beyond weight loss. Scientific research has shown that adopting a low-carb lifestyle can positively impact various aspects of your health.

- ***Weight Loss and Management:*** One of the primary reasons people turn to a low-carb diet is for its effectiveness in weight loss and weight management. When you limit your carb intake, your body enters a metabolic state called ketosis, where it efficiently burns stored fat for energy. Studies have shown that low-carb diets can lead to greater weight loss compared to low-fat diets, while also preserving lean muscle mass.

- ***Blood Sugar Control and***

Diabetes Management: Low-carb diets have been found to improve blood sugar control and insulin sensitivity, making them a valuable tool in managing and preventing type 2 diabetes. By reducing carb intake, you can avoid blood sugar spikes and support more stable blood sugar levels, reducing the need for excess insulin production.

- ***Cardiovascular Health:*** Research has indicated that low-carb diets can positively influence cardiovascular health markers. They have been shown to reduce triglyceride levels, increase levels of HDL (good) cholesterol, and improve blood pressure. These factors contribute to a decreased risk of heart disease and other cardiovascular issues.

- ***Increased Energy and Mental Clarity:*** Many individuals report experiencing improved energy levels and mental clarity when following a low-carb diet. By stabilizing blood sugar levels, you can avoid energy crashes often associated with high-carb meals. This sustained energy, coupled with the cognitive benefits of ketones as an alternative fuel source, can lead to enhanced focus, concentration, and overall mental performance.

While the scientific evidence supports the benefits of a low-carb diet, it's important to note that individual results may vary.

It's always advisable to consult with a healthcare professional or registered dietitian before making significant dietary changes, especially if you have

any underlying health conditions or are taking medications.

Common Misconceptions and Concerns

Low-carb diets have often been met with skepticism and concerns. However, many of these concerns are rooted in misconceptions or outdated information. Let's address some of the common objections:

- ***Lack of Nutritional Balance:*** Critics argue that low-carb diets may lack essential nutrients. However, with proper planning and food selection, a low-carb diet can be nutritionally balanced. By incorporating a variety of non-starchy vegetables, healthy fats, and lean proteins, you can obtain a wide range of essential vitamins, minerals, and phytonutrients.

- ***Sustainability:*** Some worry that a low-carb diet is difficult to sustain over the long term. However, with the right knowledge and recipe repertoire, low-carb eating can become a sustainable and enjoyable lifestyle. This book aims to provide you with a diverse array of recipes, meal planning strategies, and practical tips to support your long-term success.

- ***Gut Health:*** It's a common concern that reducing carb intake may negatively impact gut health due to a potential decrease in fiber consumption. While it's true that some low-carb foods may be lower in fiber, there are still plenty of low-carb options rich in fiber, such as non-starchy vegetables, nuts, and seeds. Additionally, the focus on whole, unprocessed foods in a low-carb diet can support overall gut health.

Now that we have explored the foundations and benefits of a low-carb diet, you are equipped with the knowledge to embark on this transformative journey. In the following chapters, we will dive into practical aspects of low-carb eating, including meal planning, recipe ideas, and strategies for success. Get ready to savor the delicious flavors, improve your well-being, and embrace the simplicity of a low-carb lifestyle.

Chapter 3. Meal Planning Made Easy

Let's explore now the importance of meal planning and provide you with practical strategies to make it a breeze. As following a low-carb diet can be challenging, especially for busy people, that's why meal planning is a crucial tool to help you stay on track, save time, and make healthy eating a seamless part of your lifestyle.

The Importance of Meal Planning

Meal planning is not just a mundane task; it is a powerful tool that can positively impact your life, save you money, and reduce stress. By dedicating some time to plan your meals in advance, you set yourself up for success on your low-carb journey. Here are some key benefits of meal planning:

Time Savings: By planning your meals ahead of time, you can avoid the daily dilemma of "what should I cook?" or resorting to unhealthy fast food options. With a well-thought-out plan, you'll know exactly what ingredients to buy and how to prepare your meals efficiently.

Cost-Efficiency: Meal planning allows you to make a shopping list based on your planned meals, reducing food waste and impulsive purchases. By avoiding last-minute takeout or convenience foods, you'll save money in the long run.

Dietary Adherence: Following a low-carb diet requires mindful food choices and preparation. Meal planning ensures that you have nutritious, low-carb options readily available, making it easier to stick to your dietary goals and resist temptations.

Reduced Stress: When you have your meals planned and prepped in advance, you eliminate the stress of deciding what to eat, especially during busy weekdays. You'll have the peace of mind that you're nourishing your body with healthy, balanced meals.

Key Components of a Low-Carb Meal Plan

A well-balanced low-carb meal plan consists of essential components to provide you with optimal nutrition, satiety, and enjoyment. Here are the key elements to consider when creating your low-carb meal plan:

Variety: Incorporate a diverse range of non-starchy vegetables, high-quality proteins, and healthy fats. By including a variety of colors, flavors, and textures, you'll ensure a nutritionally balanced and exciting eating experience.

Nutrient Density: Choose whole, unprocessed foods that are rich in nutrients. Focus on ingredients that provide essential vitamins, minerals, and phytonutrients, such as leafy greens, cruciferous vegetables, lean meats, fatty fish, nuts, and seeds.

Portion Control: While low-carb eating emphasizes the quality of food, it's still important to consider portion sizes. Be mindful of your portion control to avoid overeating and to maintain a healthy balance of macronutrients.

Meal Planning Strategies for Success

To make meal planning a seamless part of your routine, here are some practical strategies to help you succeed:

Set Aside Dedicated Time: Designate a specific time each week to plan your meals. This could be during the weekend or any other convenient day that works for you. Treat it as an important appointment with yourself to prioritize your health.

Create a Shopping List: Once you have planned your meals, create a shopping list based on the ingredients you'll need. Stick to the list while grocery shopping to avoid impulse purchases and ensure you have everything you need for your low-carb meals.

Consider Batch Cooking and Leftovers: Streamline your meal preparation by batch cooking certain components, such as roasted vegetables or grilled chicken, that can be used in multiple meals throughout the week. Prepare larger quantities and store leftovers for quick and easy meals on busy days.

Mindful Meal Prepping: Set aside some time to wash, chop, and prep ingredients in advance. This can include washing and storing salad greens, chopping vegetables, or marinating proteins. By having these items prepped and ready to go, you'll significantly reduce meal preparation time during the week.

Building Blocks of Low-Carb Meals

To create well-rounded and satisfying low-carb meals, it's important to incorporate the following building blocks:

Non-Starchy Vegetables: Include a generous portion of non-starchy vegetables in each meal. These include leafy greens, broccoli, cauliflower, zucchini, bell peppers, and more. These vegetables are low in carbs and packed with fiber, vitamins, and minerals, providing a range of health benefits.

Healthy Proteins: Choose lean meats, poultry, seafood, and plant-based protein sources like tofu, tempeh, and legumes. These protein sources help to build and repair tissues, support muscle development, and keep you feeling full and satisfied.

Healthy Fats: Incorporate sources of healthy fats like avocados, nuts, seeds, Extra Virgin Olive Oil, coconut oil, and fatty fish. Healthy fats not only add flavor and richness to meals but also provide important nutrients and contribute to feelings of satiety.

Customizing Your Meal Plan

While providing you with sample meal plans, we also encourage you to personalize your low-carb meal plan based on your preferences, dietary needs, and cultural considerations. The meal plans serve as a guide to help you get started and provide inspiration for creating your own meals. Feel free to make adjustments and substitutions to fit your taste and lifestyle.

Portion Control and Mindful Eating: It's important to be mindful of portion sizes and listen to your body's hunger and fullness cues.

Portion control ensures that you consume an appropriate amount of calories for your goals and helps maintain a healthy balance of nutrients.

Sample Weekly Meal Plans

At the end of this book, you will find four comprehensive weekly meal plans designed to provide you with variety, nutrition, and simplicity, making it easier for you to embrace a low-carb lifestyle.

Each meal plan includes a breakdown of breakfast, lunch, dinner, and snack options for each day of the week. We have provided detailed ingredient lists, measurements, and step-by-step instructions to make your meal preparation as smooth as possible.

Additionally, we have included variations and substitution options to accommodate different dietary restrictions or preferences. We encourage you to use these meal plans as a starting point and modify them according to your personal tastes and nutritional requirements.

By incorporating meal planning strategies and utilizing the sample meal plans provided, you will be equipped with the tools and inspiration to make low-carb eating easier than ever. Let's get ready to savor delicious meals, optimize your health, and embrace the simplicity of a low-carb diet.

Coming up in the following chapters, we will dive into specific meal ideas, recipes, and tips to make your low-carb journey even more enjoyable. Get ready to transform your eating habits and experience the incredible benefits of a low-carb lifestyle.

Chapter 4. Quick and Easy Breakfasts

Explore a variety of quick and easy breakfast options that will kick-start your day with a burst of energy and nutrition. Whether you prefer a hearty and filling meal or a lighter option to fuel your busy mornings, these recipes will provide you with delicious low-carb breakfast ideas to satisfy your taste buds and keep you on track with your health goals.

Fluffy Scrambled Eggs

Servings: 2

Preparation Time: 5 minutes

Cooking Time: 5 minutes

Ingredients:

*   4 large eggs
*   2 tablespoons heavy cream (30 ml)
*   Salt and pepper to taste
*   1 tablespoon unsalted butter (15g)
*   Fresh chives, chopped, for garnish (optional)

Instructions:

1. In a bowl, whisk together the eggs, heavy cream, salt, and pepper until well combined.
2. Heat a non-stick skillet over medium heat and add the butter. Allow it to melt and coat the bottom of the skillet evenly.
3. Pour the egg mixture into the skillet and let it cook undisturbed for a minute or two until the edges start to set.
4. Using a spatula, gently push the cooked edges toward the center, allowing the uncooked eggs to flow to the edges.
5. Continue gently stirring and folding the eggs until they are mostly cooked but still slightly runny. This will result in soft and fluffy scrambled eggs.
6. Remove the skillet from the heat and let the residual heat finish cooking the eggs to your desired doneness.
7. Serve the fluffy scrambled eggs hot, garnished with fresh chives if desired.

Nutritional Information per Serving:

*   Calories: 170
*   Proteins: 6g
*   Fats: 14g
*   Carbs: 6g
*   Fiber: 2g
*   Sugar: 2g
*   Sodium: 70mg
*   Omega 3: 0.2g

Avocado Toast with Poached Egg

Servings: 1

Preparation Time: 5 minutes

Cooking Time: 5 minutes

Ingredients:

*   1 slice of whole grain bread
*   1 ripe avocado
*   1 poached egg
*   Salt and pepper to taste
*   Red pepper flakes (optional)
*   Fresh cilantro or parsley, chopped, for garnish (optional)

Instructions:

1. Toast the bread until golden brown and crisp.
2. While the bread is toasting, cut the avocado in half and remove the pit. Scoop out the flesh and mash it with a fork until smooth.
3. Season the mashed avocado with salt and pepper to taste.
4. Prepare the poached egg by bringing a pot of water to a gentle simmer. Crack an egg into a small bowl or ramekin.
5. Create a gentle whirlpool in the simmering water and carefully slide the egg into the center of the whirlpool. Cook for about 3-4 minutes for a soft-poached egg.
6. Use a slotted spoon to carefully remove the poached egg from the water and place it on a paper towel to drain excess water.
7. Spread the mashed avocado evenly on the toasted bread.
8. Top the avocado toast with the poached egg.
9. Season with additional salt and pepper, and sprinkle with red pepper flakes and fresh cilantro or parsley if desired.

Nutritional Information per Serving:

*   Calories: 250
*   Proteins: 11g
*   Fats: 15g
*   Carbs: 19g
*   Fiber: 7g
*   Sugar: 1g
*   Sodium: 300mg
*   Omega 3: 0.2g

Greek Yogurt Parfait

Servings: 1

Preparation Time: 5 minutes

Ingredients:

- 1 cup Greek yogurt
- 1/2 cup fresh mixed berries (such as strawberries, blueberries, raspberries)
- 2 tablespoons granola
- 1 tablespoon honey (optional)
- Fresh mint leaves, for garnish (optional)

Instructions:

1. In a glass or jar, layer half of the Greek yogurt at the bottom.
2. Add a layer of fresh mixed berries on top of the yogurt.
3. Sprinkle a tablespoon of granola over the berries.
4. Repeat the layers with the remaining yogurt, berries, and granola.
5. Drizzle with honey, if desired, for added sweetness.
6. Garnish with fresh mint leaves for an extra touch of freshness.
7. Serve immediately and enjoy!

Nutritional Information per Serving:

- Calories: 220
- Proteins: 20g
- Fats: 5g
- Carbs: 25g
- Fiber: 4g
- Sugar: 15g
- Sodium: 60mg
- Omega 3: 0.1g

Spinach and Feta Omelette

Servings: 1

Preparation Time: 5 minutes

Cooking Time: 5 minutes

Ingredients:

- 3 large eggs
- 1/2 cup fresh spinach leaves
- 1/4 cup crumbled feta cheese
- Salt and pepper to taste
- 1 tablespoon Extra Virgin Olive Oil

Instructions:

1. In a bowl, whisk the eggs until well beaten. Season with salt and pepper.
2. Heat olive oil in a non-stick skillet over medium heat.
3. Add the fresh spinach leaves to the skillet and sauté for a minute until wilted.
4. Pour the beaten eggs into the skillet, evenly distributing them over the spinach.
5. Allow the eggs to cook undisturbed for a minute until the edges start to set.
6. Sprinkle the crumbled feta cheese evenly over one half of the omelette.
7. Using a spatula, gently fold the other half of the omelette over the filling.
8. Cook for another minute or until the eggs are fully cooked and the cheese has melted.
9. Carefully slide the omelette onto a plate and serve hot.

Nutritional Information per Serving:

- Calories: 280
- Proteins: 23g
- Fats: 20g
- Carbs: 3g
- Fiber: 1g
- Sugar: 1g
- Sodium: 490mg
- Omega 3: 0.4g

Blueberry Almond Chia Pudding

Servings: 1

Preparation Time: 5 minutes Chilling Time: 4 hours or overnight

Ingredients:

- 2 tablespoons chia seeds
- 1/2 cup almond milk (unsweetened)
- 1/4 teaspoon vanilla extract
- 1/2 cup fresh blueberries
- 1 tablespoon sliced almonds
- 1 teaspoon honey or maple syrup (optional)

Instructions:

1.   In a bowl or jar, combine chia seeds, almond milk, and vanilla extract. Stir well to ensure the chia seeds are evenly distributed.
2.   Let the mixture sit for 5 minutes, then give it another stir to prevent clumping.
3.   Cover the bowl or jar and refrigerate for at least 4 hours or overnight to allow the chia seeds to absorb the liquid and create a pudding-like consistency.
4.   Before serving, give the chia pudding a good stir to break up any clumps that may have formed.
5.   Layer the chia pudding with fresh blueberries in a serving glass or jar.
6.   Top with sliced almonds for added crunch and texture.
7.   If desired, drizzle with a teaspoon of honey or maple syrup for sweetness.
8.   Enjoy the Blueberry Almond Chia Pudding chilled.

Nutritional Information per Serving:

- Calories: 220
- Proteins: 7g
- Fats: 12g
- Carbs: 25g
- Fiber: 11g
- Sugar: 10g
- Sodium: 90mg
- Omega 3: 3g

Breakfast Burrito

Servings: 1

Preparation Time: 10 minutes Cooking Time: 10 minutes

Ingredients:

- 2 large eggs
- 2 tablespoons milk
- 1/4 cup diced bell peppers (any color)
- 1/4 cup diced onions
- 2 slices of turkey bacon, cooked and crumbled
- 1/4 cup shredded cheddar cheese
- Salt and pepper to taste
- 1 large whole wheat tortilla
- Salsa or hot sauce for serving (optional)

Instructions:

1.   In a bowl, whisk together the eggs and milk. Season with salt and pepper.
2.   Heat a non-stick skillet over medium heat and spray with cooking spray.
3.   Add the diced bell peppers and onions to the skillet and sauté until they soften, about 3-4 minutes.
4.   Pour the beaten eggs into the skillet with the peppers and onions. Cook, stirring occasionally, until the eggs are scrambled and cooked through.
5.   Sprinkle the crumbled turkey bacon and shredded cheddar cheese over the eggs. Stir to combine and allow the cheese to melt.
6.   Warm the whole wheat tortilla in a separate skillet or microwave until pliable.
7.   Spoon the egg mixture onto the tortilla and fold in the sides to form a burrito.
8.   Serve the breakfast burrito with salsa or hot sauce on the side, if desired.

Nutritional Information per Serving:

- Calories: 370
- Proteins: 26g
- Fats: 20g
- Carbs: 26g
- Fiber: 5g
- Sugar: 4g
- Sodium: 640mg
- Omega 3: 0.4g

Smoked Salmon and Cream Cheese Bagel

Servings: 1

Preparation Time: 5 minutes

Ingredients:

- 1 whole wheat bagel
- 2 tablespoons cream cheese
- 2 ounces smoked salmon
- Thinly sliced red onion
- Capers, for garnish
- Fresh dill, for garnish
- Lemon wedges, for serving

Instructions:

1. Slice the whole wheat bagel in half horizontally.
2. Spread the cream cheese evenly on both halves of the bagel.
3. Layer the smoked salmon on the bottom half of the bagel.
4. Top with thinly sliced red onion, capers, and fresh dill.
5. Squeeze a lemon wedge over the salmon for added freshness.
6. Place the top half of the bagel on the salmon to create a sandwich.
7. Serve the Smoked Salmon and Cream Cheese Bagel immediately.

Nutritional Information per Serving:

- Calories: 390
- Proteins: 25g
- Fats: 10g
- Carbs: 49g
- Fiber: 7g
- Sugar: 5g
- Sodium: 820mg
- Omega 3: 1.5g

Vegetable Frittata

Servings: 2-3

Preparation Time: 10 minutes

Cooking Time: 15 minutes

Ingredients:

- 6 large eggs
- 1/4 cup milk
- 1 tablespoon Extra Virgin Olive Oil
- 1/2 cup diced bell peppers (any color)
- 1/2 cup diced zucchini
- 1/2 cup diced cherry tomatoes
- 1/4 cup diced red onion
- 1/4 cup shredded cheddar cheese
- Salt and pepper to taste
- Fresh herbs (such as parsley or basil) for garnish (optional)

Instructions:

1. Preheat the oven to 375°F (190°C).
2. In a bowl, whisk together the eggs and milk. Season with salt and pepper.
3. Heat olive oil in an oven-safe skillet over medium heat.
4. Add the diced bell peppers, zucchini, cherry tomatoes, and red onion to the skillet. Sauté until the vegetables soften, about 5-6 minutes.
5. Pour the egg mixture into the skillet, ensuring it evenly covers the vegetables.
6. Sprinkle the shredded cheddar cheese over the top of the frittata.
7. Transfer the skillet to the preheated oven and bake for about 12-15 minutes, or until the eggs are set and the cheese is melted and slightly golden.
8. Remove from the oven and let the frittata cool slightly.
9. Cut into wedges and garnish with fresh herbs, if desired.
10. Serve the Vegetable Frittata warm.

Nutritional Information per Serving (based on 3 servings):

- Calories: 210
- Proteins: 14g
- Fats: 14g
- Carbs: 7g
- Fiber: 2g
- Sugar: 4g
- Sodium: 280mg
- Omega 3: 0.5g

Overnight Oats

Servings: 1

Preparation Time: 5 minutes

Chilling Time: Overnight

Ingredients:

- 1/2 cup rolled oats
- 1/2 cup almond milk (unsweetened)
- 1 tablespoon chia seeds
- 1 tablespoon honey or maple syrup
- 1/4 teaspoon vanilla extract
- Fresh fruits (such as berries or sliced banana) for topping
- Nuts or seeds (such as sliced almonds or pumpkin seeds) for topping
- Cinnamon or nutmeg for flavor (optional)

Instructions:

1. In a jar or container with a lid, combine rolled oats, almond milk, chia seeds, honey or maple syrup, and vanilla extract.
2. Stir well to ensure all the ingredients are well combined.
3. Cover the jar or container and refrigerate overnight or for at least 6-8 hours to allow the oats and chia seeds to soften and absorb the liquid.
4. In the morning, give the mixture a good stir.
5. If desired, add a sprinkle of cinnamon or nutmeg for added flavor.
6. Top with fresh fruits and nuts or seeds of your choice.
7. Enjoy the Overnight Oats chilled.

Nutritional Information per Serving:

- Calories: 320
- Proteins: 9g
- Fats: 11g
- Carbs: 49g
- Fiber: 11g
- Sugar: 15g
- Sodium: 100mg
- Omega 3: 2g

Banana Nut Pancakes

Servings: 2-3

Preparation Time: 10 minutes

Cooking Time: 10 minutes

Ingredients:

- 1 cup whole wheat flour
- 1 tablespoon baking powder
- 1/4 teaspoon salt
- 1 ripe banana, mashed
- 1 cup almond milk (unsweetened)
- 1 tablespoon maple syrup
- 1/2 teaspoon vanilla extract
- 1/4 cup chopped walnuts
- Cooking spray or oil for greasing the pan
- Sliced bananas and additional chopped walnuts for serving (optional)

Instructions:

1. In a large bowl, whisk together the whole wheat flour, baking powder, and salt.
2. In a separate bowl, combine the mashed banana, almond milk, maple syrup, and vanilla extract. Mix well.
3. Pour the wet ingredients into the dry ingredients and stir until just combined. Do not overmix.
4. Gently fold in the chopped walnuts.
5. Heat a non-stick skillet or griddle over medium heat and lightly grease it with cooking spray or oil.
6. Pour 1/4 cup of the pancake batter onto the skillet for each pancake.
7. Cook until bubbles form on the surface of the pancakes, then flip and cook the other side until golden brown.
8. Repeat with the remaining batter.
9. Serve the Banana Nut Pancakes with sliced bananas and additional chopped walnuts, if desired.

Nutritional Information per Serving (based on 3 servings):

- Calories: 280
- Proteins: 8g
- Fats: 10g
- Carbs: 44g
- Fiber: 7g
- Sugar: 10g
- Sodium: 370mg
- Omega 3: 1g

Peanut Butter Banana Smoothie

Servings: 1

Preparation Time: 5 minutes

Ingredients:

- 1 ripe banana
- 1 cup almond milk (unsweetened)
- 1 tablespoon peanut butter
- 1 tablespoon honey or maple syrup
- 1/2 teaspoon vanilla extract
- 1/2 cup ice cubes

Instructions:

1. Peel the ripe banana and break it into smaller pieces.
2. In a blender, combine the banana, almond milk, peanut butter, honey or maple syrup, vanilla extract, and ice cubes.
3. Blend on high speed until all the ingredients are well combined and the smoothie is creamy and smooth.
4. If desired, add more almond milk or ice cubes to adjust the consistency.
5. Pour the Peanut Butter Banana Smoothie into a glass and serve immediately.

Nutritional Information per Serving:

- Calories: 280
- Proteins: 8g
- Fats: 12g
- Carbs: 39g
- Fiber: 4g
- Sugar: 23g
- Sodium: 150mg
- Omega 3: 0g

Veggie Breakfast Casserole

Servings: 4-6

Preparation Time: 15 minutes

Cooking Time: 30 minutes

Ingredients:

- 6 large eggs
- 1 cup milk (any type, such as almond or dairy milk)
- 1 tablespoon olive oil
- 1 small onion, diced
- 1 bell pepper, diced
- 1 zucchini, diced
- 1 cup sliced mushrooms
- 2 cups baby spinach
- 1 cup shredded cheddar cheese
- Salt and pepper to taste
- Fresh herbs (such as parsley or chives) for garnish (optional)

Instructions:

1. Preheat the oven to 375°F (190°C). Grease a baking dish with olive oil or cooking spray.
2. In a large bowl, whisk together the eggs and milk. Season with salt and pepper.
3. Heat olive oil in a skillet over medium heat. Add the diced onion, bell pepper, zucchini, and mushrooms. Sauté until the vegetables are tender, about 5-6 minutes.
4. Add the baby spinach to the skillet and cook until wilted, about 2 minutes.
5. Transfer the sautéed vegetables to the greased baking dish and spread them out evenly.
6. Pour the egg mixture over the vegetables in the baking dish.
7. Sprinkle the shredded cheddar cheese over the top of the casserole.
8. Bake in the preheated oven for about 25-30 minutes, or until the eggs are set and the cheese is melted and slightly golden.
9. Remove from the oven and let the casserole cool slightly.
10. Garnish with fresh herbs, if desired, and serve the Veggie Breakfast Casserole warm.

Nutritional Information per Serving
(based on 6 servings):

- Calories: 230
- Proteins: 14g
- Fats: 15g
- Carbs: 10g
- Fiber: 2g
- Sugar: 4g
- Sodium: 320mg
- Omega 3: 0.5g

Sausage and Egg Muffins

Servings: 4-6

Preparation Time: 10 minutes

Cooking Time: 20 minutes

Ingredients:

- 6 eggs
- 1/4 cup milk (any type, such as almond or dairy milk)
- 1/2 lb ground sausage
- 1/2 cup diced bell peppers
- 1/2 cup diced onions
- 1/2 cup shredded cheddar cheese
- Salt and pepper to taste
- Cooking spray for greasing the muffin tin

Instructions:

1. Preheat the oven to 375°F (190°C). Grease a muffin tin with cooking spray.
2. In a large bowl, whisk together the eggs and milk. Season with salt and pepper.
3. In a skillet, cook the ground sausage over medium heat until browned and cooked through. Remove from heat and drain any excess grease.
4. In the same skillet, sauté the diced bell peppers and onions until softened.
5. Add the cooked sausage to the skillet with the sautéed vegetables and mix well.
6. Divide the sausage and vegetable mixture evenly among the muffin cups in the greased muffin tin.
7. Pour the egg mixture over the sausage and vegetables in each muffin cup, filling them about three-fourths full.
8. Sprinkle shredded cheddar cheese on top of each muffin cup.
9. Bake in the preheated oven for about 15-20 minutes, or until the eggs are set and the cheese is melted and slightly golden.
10. Remove from the oven and let the muffins cool for a few minutes before serving.

Nutritional Information per Serving
(based on 6 servings):

- Calories: 240
- Proteins: 14g
- Fats: 18g
- Carbs: 3g
- Fiber: 0g
- Sugar: 1g
- Sodium: 380mg
- Omega 3: 0.4g

Berry Protein Pancakes

Servings: 2

Preparation Time: 10 minutes

Cooking Time: 10 minutes

Ingredients:

*   1 cup oats
*   1 ripe banana
*   2 eggs
*   1/2 cup Greek yogurt
*   1/2 teaspoon baking powder
*   1/2 teaspoon vanilla extract
*   1/2 cup mixed berries (such as blueberries, raspberries, or strawberries)
*   Cooking spray or butter for greasing the pan
*   Optional toppings: additional berries, Greek yogurt, honey, or maple syrup

Instructions:

1.   In a blender or food processor, blend the oats until they reach a flour-like consistency.
2.   In a mixing bowl, mash the ripe banana with a fork until smooth.
3.   Add the eggs, Greek yogurt, blended oats, baking powder, and vanilla extract to the bowl. Mix well until all the ingredients are combined.
4.   Gently fold in the mixed berries into the pancake batter.
5.   Heat a non-stick skillet or griddle over medium heat and lightly grease it with cooking spray or butter.
6.   Pour about 1/4 cup of the pancake batter onto the skillet for each pancake. Cook until bubbles form on the surface, then flip and cook the other side until golden brown.
7.   Repeat the process with the remaining batter.
8.   Serve the Berry Protein Pancakes warm, topped with additional berries, Greek yogurt, honey, or maple syrup if desired.

Nutritional Information per Serving
(based on 2 servings):

*   Calories: 340
*   Proteins: 19g
*   Fats: 8g
*   Carbs: 51g
*   Fiber: 7g
*   Sugar: 14g
*   Sodium: 140mg
*   Omega 3: 0.3g

Breakfast Quiche Cups

Servings: 6

Preparation Time: 10 minutes

Cooking Time: 20 minutes

Ingredients:

*   6 large eggs
*   1/2 cup milk (any type, such as almond or dairy milk)
*   1 cup chopped vegetables (such as spinach, bell peppers, mushrooms, or onions)
*   1/2 cup shredded cheddar cheese
*   4-6 slices of cooked bacon, crumbled
*   Salt and pepper to taste
*   Cooking spray for greasing the muffin tin

Instructions:

1.   Preheat the oven to 375°F (190°C). Grease a muffin tin with cooking spray.
2.   In a bowl, whisk together the eggs and milk. Season with salt and pepper.
3.   Divide the chopped vegetables evenly among the muffin cups in the greased muffin tin.
4.   Sprinkle shredded cheddar cheese on top of the vegetables in each muffin cup.
5.   Pour the egg mixture over the vegetables and cheese in each muffin cup, filling them about three-fourths full.
6.   Sprinkle the crumbled bacon on top of each muffin cup.
7.   Bake in the preheated oven for about 15-20 minutes, or until the eggs are set and the quiche cups are lightly golden.
8.   Remove from the oven and let the quiche cups cool for a few minutes before serving.

Nutritional Information per Serving
(based on 6 servings):

- Calories: 160
- Proteins: 12g
- Fats: 10g
- Carbs: 4g
- Fiber: 1g
- Sugar: 1g
- Sodium: 240mg
- Omega 3: 0.2g

Breakfast Burrito Bowl

Servings: 2

Preparation Time: 10 minutes

Cooking Time: 10 minutes

Ingredients:

- 4 large eggs
- 1 tablespoon olive oil
- 1/2 cup diced bell peppers
- 1/2 cup diced onions
- 1 cup cooked quinoa
- 1 cup black beans, drained and rinsed
- 1/2 cup diced tomatoes
- 1/4 cup chopped fresh cilantro
- 1/4 cup shredded cheddar cheese
- Salt and pepper to taste
- Optional toppings: avocado slices, salsa, Greek yogurt, or hot sauce

Instructions:

1. In a bowl, whisk the eggs together and season with salt and pepper.
2. Heat olive oil in a skillet over medium heat. Add the diced bell peppers and onions and sauté until softened.
3. Pour the whisked eggs into the skillet with the sautéed vegetables. Cook, stirring occasionally, until the eggs are scrambled and cooked to your desired consistency.
4. Divide the cooked quinoa into two bowls.
5. Top each bowl with half of the scrambled eggs, black beans, diced tomatoes, fresh cilantro, and shredded cheddar cheese.
6. Add any optional toppings such as avocado slices, salsa, Greek yogurt, or hot sauce.
7. Serve the Breakfast Burrito Bowl warm and enjoy!

Nutritional Information per Serving
(based on 2 servings):

- Calories: 400
- Proteins: 23g
- Fats: 16g
- Carbs: 42g
- Fiber: 10g
- Sugar: 4g
- Sodium: 360mg
- Omega 3: 0.3g

Chia Seed Pudding with Berries

Servings: 2

Preparation Time: 5 minutes

Refrigeration Time: 4 hours or overnight

Ingredients:

- 1/4 cup chia seeds
- 1 cup unsweetened almond milk (or any other milk of your choice)
- 1 tablespoon maple syrup or honey (optional)
- 1/2 teaspoon vanilla extract
- 1/2 cup mixed berries (such as strawberries, blueberries, or raspberries)
- Optional toppings: additional berries, nuts, or shredded coconut

Instructions:

1. In a bowl, whisk together the chia seeds, almond milk, maple syrup or honey (if using), and vanilla extract.
2. Let the mixture sit for a few minutes to allow the chia seeds to absorb the liquid, then whisk again to ensure they are evenly distributed.
3. Cover the bowl and refrigerate for at least 4 hours or overnight, until the chia pudding has thickened and set.
4. Once the chia pudding has set, give it a good stir to break up any clumps.

5. Divide the chia seed pudding into two serving bowls or jars.
6. Top the pudding with mixed berries and any other desired toppings, such as additional berries, nuts, or shredded coconut.
7. Serve the Chia Seed Pudding with Berries chilled and enjoy!

Nutritional Information per Serving
(based on 2 servings):

- Calories: 160
- Proteins: 5g
- Fats: 9g
- Carbs: 16g
- Fiber: 12g
- Sugar: 3g
- Sodium: 80mg
- Omega 3: 2.5g

Sweet Potato Hash with Eggs

Servings: 2

Preparation Time: 10 minutes

Cooking Time: 15 minutes

Ingredients:

- 2 cups diced sweet potatoes
- 1 tablespoon olive oil
- 1/2 cup diced onions
- 1/2 cup diced bell peppers
- 2 cloves garlic, minced
- 1/2 teaspoon paprika
- 1/2 teaspoon dried thyme
- Salt and pepper to taste
- 4 large eggs
- Fresh parsley for garnish (optional)

Instructions:

1. In a large skillet, heat olive oil over medium heat.
2. Add the diced sweet potatoes and cook until they are tender and lightly browned, about 8-10 minutes.
3. Add the diced onions, bell peppers, and minced garlic to the skillet. Cook for another 2-3 minutes until the vegetables are softened.
4. Sprinkle the paprika, dried thyme, salt, and pepper over the sweet potato mixture. Stir well to combine the flavors.
5. Create 4 wells in the sweet potato hash and crack an egg into each well.
6. Cover the skillet with a lid and cook for about 5-6 minutes, or until the eggs are cooked to your desired doneness.
7. Remove from heat and garnish with fresh parsley if desired.
8. Serve the Sweet Potato Hash with Eggs hot and enjoy!

Nutritional Information per Serving
(based on 2 servings):

- Calories: 280
- Proteins: 12g
- Fats: 11g
- Carbs: 37g
- Fiber: 6g
- Sugar: 9g
- Sodium: 240mg
- Omega 3: 0.4g

Omelette Muffins

Servings: 4 (2 muffins per serving)

Preparation Time: 10 minutes

Cooking Time: 20 minutes

Ingredients:

- 6 large eggs
- 1/4 cup milk
- 1/2 cup diced bell peppers
- 1/2 cup diced onions
- 1/2 cup diced tomatoes
- 1/4 cup chopped spinach
- 1/4 cup shredded cheddar cheese
- Salt and pepper to taste
- Cooking spray

Instructions:

1. Preheat the oven to 350°F (175°C). Grease a muffin tin with cooking spray.
2. In a bowl, whisk together the eggs and milk until well combined.
3. Stir in the diced bell peppers, onions, tomatoes, chopped spinach, shredded cheddar cheese, salt, and pepper.
4. Pour the egg mixture evenly into the greased muffin tin, filling each cup about 3/4 full.
5. Bake in the preheated oven for 18-20 minutes, or until the omelette muffins are set and slightly golden on top.
6. Remove from the oven and let cool for a few minutes.
7. Use a butter knife to gently loosen the edges of the muffins, then transfer them to a wire rack to cool completely.
8. Serve the Omelette Muffins as a delicious and convenient breakfast or snack option.

Nutritional Information per Serving (2 muffins):

- Calories: 170
- Proteins: 12g
- Fats: 11g
- Carbs: 5g
- Fiber: 1g
- Sugar: 2g
- Sodium: 250mg
- Omega 3: 0.3g

Almond Flour Pancakes

Servings: 2 (2-3 pancakes per serving)

Preparation Time: 10 minutes

Cooking Time: 10 minutes

Ingredients:

- 1 cup almond flour
- 2 tablespoons coconut flour
- 1 teaspoon baking powder
- 1/4 teaspoon salt
- 1/2 teaspoon ground cinnamon (optional)
- 2 large eggs
- 1/4 cup unsweetened almond milk (or any other milk of your choice)
- 1 tablespoon maple syrup or honey (optional)
- 1/2 teaspoon vanilla extract
- Cooking oil or butter for greasing the pan
- Toppings of your choice: fresh berries, sliced bananas, nuts, or a drizzle of maple syrup

Instructions:

1. In a mixing bowl, whisk together the almond flour, coconut flour, baking powder, salt, and ground cinnamon (if using).
2. In a separate bowl, whisk together the eggs, almond milk, maple syrup or honey (if using), and vanilla extract until well combined.
3. Pour the wet ingredients into the dry ingredients and whisk until a smooth batter forms. Let the batter rest for a few minutes to thicken.
4. Heat a non-stick skillet or griddle over medium heat and lightly grease with cooking oil or butter.
5. Spoon about 1/4 cup of the batter onto the skillet for each pancake. Use the back of the spoon to spread the batter into a circular shape.
6. Cook the pancakes for 2-3 minutes, or until bubbles start to form on the surface. Flip the pancakes and cook for an additional 1-2 minutes, until golden brown and cooked through.
7. Repeat the process with the remaining batter, greasing the skillet as

needed.

8.   Serve the Almond Flour Pancakes warm with your favorite toppings, such as fresh berries, sliced bananas, nuts, or a drizzle of maple syrup.

Nutritional Information per Serving
(2-3 pancakes):

- Calories: 280
- Proteins: 12g
- Fats: 22g
- Carbs: 10g
- Fiber: 5g
- Sugar: 2g
- Sodium: 280mg
- Omega 3: 0.5g

Chapter 5. Simple Lunches on the Go

In this Chapter we'll focus on simple lunches that you can enjoy on the go. We understand that busy schedules often leave little time for elaborate meal preparations, especially during the lunch hour. That's why we've curated a collection of delicious and hassle-free recipes that are perfect for those on the move.

In this chapter, you'll find a variety of lunch options that are easy to prepare, portable, and packed with nutrients. Whether you're heading to work, school, or simply need a quick bite while running errands, these recipes will satisfy your hunger and keep you fueled throughout the day.

We've carefully selected a range of US and UK-inspired recipes, as well as Mediterranean-inspired ones, to cater to different tastes and preferences. From wraps and salads to hearty sandwiches and protein-packed bowls, you'll find a lunch option to suit your needs and dietary goals.

So, let's dive in and discover the joy of simple lunches on the go. Say goodbye to dull and uninspiring midday meals and embrace the convenience and deliciousness of these quick and nourishing recipes.

Chicken Caesar Salad Wrap

Servings: 2

Preparation Time: 10 minutes

Ingredients:

- 2 large whole wheat or low-carb tortillas
- 2 cups cooked chicken breast, shredded or sliced
- 2 cups romaine lettuce, chopped
- 1/4 cup grated Parmesan cheese
- 1/4 cup Caesar dressing (homemade or store-bought)
- Salt and pepper to taste

Instructions:

1. Lay the tortillas flat on a clean surface.
2. In the center of each tortilla, layer the cooked chicken breast, romaine lettuce, grated Parmesan cheese, and Caesar dressing.
3. Season with salt and pepper to taste.
4. Fold the sides of the tortilla inward, then tightly roll it up from the bottom, making sure the filling is secure.
5. Cut the wrap in half diagonally to create two portions.
6. Serve the Chicken Caesar Salad Wrap immediately or wrap it tightly in foil for later enjoyment.

Nutritional Information per Serving:

- Calories: 400
- Proteins: 35g
- Fats: 18g
- Carbs: 25g
- Fiber: 5g
- Sugar: 2g
- Sodium: 720mg
- Omega 3: 0.3g

Sahara's Hummus Wrap

Servings: 2

Preparation Time: 10 minutes

Ingredients:

- 2 large whole wheat or low-carb tortillas
- 1 cup hummus
- 1 cup cucumber, thinly sliced
- 1 cup cherry tomatoes, halved
- 1/4 cup Kalamata olives, pitted and sliced
- 1/4 cup crumbled feta cheese
- 2 tablespoons fresh parsley, chopped
- Salt and pepper to taste

Instructions:

1. Lay the tortillas flat on a clean surface.
2. Spread a generous amount of hummus onto each tortilla, covering the entire surface.
3. Layer the cucumber slices, cherry tomatoes, Kalamata olives, crumbled feta cheese, and fresh parsley evenly on top of the hummus.
4. Season with salt and pepper to taste.
5. Roll the tortilla tightly, starting from one end, to create a wrap.
6. Cut the wrap in half diagonally to create two portions.
7. Serve the Mediterranean Hummus Wrap immediately or wrap it tightly in foil for later consumption.

Nutritional Information per Serving:

- Calories: 350
- Proteins: 10g
- Fats: 15g
- Carbs: 45g
- Fiber: 8g
- Sugar: 3g
- Sodium: 550mg
- Omega 3: 0.1g

Mediterranean Chicken Pita Pocket

Servings: 2

Preparation Time: 10 minutes

Ingredients:

- 2 whole wheat pita breads
- 1 cup cooked chicken breast, shredded or sliced
- 1/2 cup cherry tomatoes, halved
- 1/4 cup diced cucumber
- 1/4 cup diced red onion
- 1/4 cup Kalamata olives, pitted and sliced
- 2 tablespoons crumbled feta cheese
- 2 tablespoons fresh parsley, chopped
- 2 tablespoons Greek yogurt
- Juice of 1/2 lemon
- Salt and pepper to taste

Instructions:

1. Cut the pita breads in half to create pockets.
2. In a mixing bowl, combine the cooked chicken breast, cherry tomatoes, diced cucumber, diced red onion, Kalamata olives, crumbled feta cheese, and fresh parsley.
3. In a small bowl, whisk together the Greek yogurt, lemon juice, salt, and pepper to create a dressing.
4. Pour the dressing over the chicken and vegetable mixture and toss until well coated.
5. Stuff each pita pocket with the Mediterranean chicken and vegetable mixture.
6. Serve the Mediterranean Chicken Pita Pockets immediately or wrap them tightly in foil for later enjoyment.

Nutritional Information per Serving:

- Calories: 350
- Proteins: 20g
- Fats: 8g
- Carbs: 45g
- Fiber: 6g
- Sugar: 4g
- Sodium: 500mg
- Omega 3: 0.2g

Greek Pasta Salad

Servings: 4

Preparation Time: 15 minutes

Cooking Time: 10 minutes

Ingredients:

- 8 oz whole wheat pasta (such as penne or fusilli)
- 1 cup cherry tomatoes, halved
- 1/2 cup cucumber, diced
- 1/4 cup red onion, thinly sliced
- 1/4 cup Kalamata olives, pitted and halved
- 1/4 cup crumbled feta cheese
- 2 tablespoons fresh parsley, chopped
- 2 tablespoons fresh dill, chopped
- 2 tablespoons Extra Virgin Olive Oil
- 1 tablespoon lemon juice
- 1 teaspoon dried oregano
- Salt and pepper to taste

Instructions:

1. Cook the pasta according to the package instructions until al dente. Drain and rinse with cold water to cool it down.
2. In a large mixing bowl, combine the cooked pasta, cherry tomatoes, cucumber, red onion, Kalamata olives, crumbled feta cheese, fresh parsley, and fresh dill.
3. In a small bowl, whisk together the Extra Virgin Olive Oil, lemon juice, dried oregano, salt, and pepper to create a dressing.
4. Pour the dressing over the pasta and vegetable mixture and toss until well coated.
5. Adjust the seasoning if needed.
6. Serve the Greek Pasta Salad immediately or refrigerate for a couple of hours to allow the flavors to meld together.

Nutritional Information per Serving:

- Calories: 250
- Proteins: 8g
- Fats: 8g
- Carbs: 38g
- Fiber: 5g
- Sugar: 3g
- Sodium: 250mg

Quinoa Stuffed Bell Peppers

Servings: 4

Preparation Time: 20 minutes

Cooking Time: 30 minutes

Ingredients:

- 4 bell peppers (any color)
- 1 cup cooked quinoa
- 1/2 cup black beans, rinsed and drained
- 1/2 cup corn kernels
- 1/2 cup diced tomatoes
- 1/4 cup diced red onion
- 1/4 cup chopped fresh cilantro
- 1/2 teaspoon ground cumin
- 1/2 teaspoon chili powder
- 1/4 teaspoon garlic powder
- Salt and pepper to taste
- 1/2 cup shredded cheddar cheese (optional)

Instructions:

1. Preheat the oven to 375°F (190°C).
2. Slice the tops off the bell peppers and remove the seeds and membranes. Place the bell peppers in a baking dish and set aside.
3. In a mixing bowl, combine the cooked quinoa, black beans, corn kernels, diced tomatoes, red onion, chopped cilantro, ground cumin, chili powder, garlic powder, salt, and pepper. Mix well to combine.
4. Spoon the quinoa mixture into the bell peppers, filling them to the top.
5. If desired, sprinkle shredded cheddar cheese on top of each stuffed bell pepper.
6. Cover the baking dish with foil and bake for 25-30 minutes, or until the bell peppers are tender and the filling is heated through.
7. Remove from the oven and let cool for a few minutes before serving.

Nutritional Information per Serving:

- Calories: 200
- Proteins: 8g
- Fats: 3g
- Carbs: 40g
- Fiber: 8g
- Sugar: 5g
- Sodium: 200mg
- Omega 3: 0.1g

Turkey and Cranberry Salad Wrap

Servings: 4

Preparation Time: 15 minutes

Ingredients:

- 2 cups cooked turkey breast, shredded
- 1/2 cup dried cranberries
- 1/4 cup chopped pecans
- 1/4 cup diced celery
- 1/4 cup plain Greek yogurt
- 1 tablespoon mayonnaise
- 1 tablespoon Dijon mustard
- 1 tablespoon fresh lemon juice
- Salt and pepper to taste
- 4 large whole wheat tortillas
- 2 cups mixed salad greens

Instructions:

1. In a large mixing bowl, combine the shredded turkey breast, dried cranberries, chopped pecans, diced celery, Greek yogurt, mayonnaise, Dijon mustard, fresh lemon juice, salt, and pepper. Mix well to combine.
2. Lay out the whole wheat tortillas and divide the turkey and cranberry salad mixture evenly among them, spreading it out in a line down the center of each tortilla.
3. Top the salad mixture with a handful of mixed salad greens.
4. Roll up the tortillas tightly, tucking in the sides as you go, to create wraps.
5. Slice the wraps in half diagonally, if desired, and serve.

Nutritional Information per Serving:

- Calories: 320
- Proteins: 25g
- Fats: 10g
- Carbs: 35g
- Fiber: 6g
- Sugar: 12g
- Sodium: 280mg
- Omega 3: 0.2g

Caprese Chicken Salad

Servings: 4

Preparation Time: 15 minutes

Cooking Time: 20 minutes

Ingredients:

- 2 boneless, skinless chicken breasts
- Salt and pepper to taste
- 2 tablespoons olive oil
- 2 cups cherry tomatoes, halved
- 8 ounces fresh mozzarella cheese, sliced
- 1/4 cup fresh basil leaves, torn
- Balsamic glaze, for drizzling

Instructions:

1. Season the chicken breasts with salt and pepper on both sides.
2. In a large skillet, heat the olive oil over medium heat. Add the chicken breasts and cook for about 8-10 minutes per side, or until cooked through and no longer pink in the center. Remove from the skillet and let cool for a few minutes.
3. Slice the cooked chicken breasts into thin strips.
4. Arrange the cherry tomatoes, fresh mozzarella slices, and sliced chicken on a serving platter or individual plates.
5. Sprinkle torn basil leaves over the salad.
6. Drizzle balsamic glaze over the salad for added flavor.
7. Serve immediately and enjoy.

Nutritional Information per Serving:

- Calories: 320
- Proteins: 30g
- Fats: 18g
- Carbs: 8g
- Fiber: 1g
- Sugar: 4g
- Sodium: 320mg
- Omega 3: 0.1g

Veggie Hummus Wrap

Servings: 4

Preparation Time: 10 minutes

Ingredients:

- 4 large whole wheat tortillas
- 1/2 cup hummus
- 1 cup mixed salad greens
- 1/2 cup thinly sliced cucumber
- 1/2 cup shredded carrots
- 1/2 cup sliced bell peppers
- 1/4 cup sliced red onion
- 1/4 cup crumbled feta cheese (optional)
- Salt and pepper to taste

Instructions:

1. Lay out the whole wheat tortillas and spread a generous amount of hummus onto each tortilla.
2. Layer the mixed salad greens, sliced cucumber, shredded carrots, sliced bell peppers, red onion, and crumbled feta cheese (if using) evenly on top of the hummus.
3. Season with salt and pepper to taste.
4. Roll up the tortillas tightly, tucking in the sides as you go, to create wraps.
5. Slice the wraps in half diagonally, if desired, and serve.

Nutritional Information per Serving:

- Calories: 250
- Proteins: 8g
- Fats: 10g
- Carbs: 35g
- Fiber: 6g
- Sugar: 3g
- Sodium: 320mg
- Omega 3: 0.2g

Greek Chickpea Salad

Servings: 4

Preparation Time: 15 minutes

Ingredients:

- 2 cups cooked chickpeas
- 1 cup cherry tomatoes, halved
- 1 cucumber, diced
- 1/2 red onion, thinly sliced
- 1/2 cup Kalamata olives, pitted and halved
- 1/2 cup crumbled feta cheese
- 1/4 cup chopped fresh parsley
- 2 tablespoons Extra Virgin Olive Oil
- 2 tablespoons lemon juice
- 1 teaspoon dried oregano
- Salt and pepper to taste

Instructions:

1. In a large mixing bowl, combine the cooked chickpeas, cherry tomatoes, cucumber, red onion, Kalamata olives, crumbled feta cheese, and chopped fresh parsley.
2. In a small bowl, whisk together the Extra Virgin Olive Oil, lemon juice, dried oregano, salt, and pepper to make the dressing.
3. Pour the dressing over the chickpea mixture and toss well to coat all the ingredients.
4. Adjust the seasoning with additional salt and pepper, if desired.
5. Let the salad marinate in the refrigerator for at least 30 minutes to allow the flavors to meld together.
6. Serve chilled and enjoy.

Nutritional Information per Serving:

- Calories: 280
- Proteins: 10g
- Fats: 12g
- Carbs: 32g
- Fiber: 8g
- Sugar: 6g
- Sodium: 480mg
- Omega 3: 0.2g

Falafel Wrap

Servings: 4

Preparation Time: 15 minutes

Ingredients:

- 4 whole wheat wraps or pita bread
- 16 homemade or store-bought falafel balls
- 1 cup chopped lettuce
- 1/2 cup diced tomatoes
- 1/2 cup diced cucumbers
- 1/4 cup chopped red onion
- 1/4 cup chopped fresh parsley
- 1/4 cup crumbled feta cheese
- Tzatziki sauce for serving (optional)

Instructions:

1. Warm the whole wheat wraps or pita bread according to package instructions to make them more pliable.
2. Place 4 falafel balls in the center of each wrap.
3. Top the falafel with chopped lettuce, diced tomatoes, diced cucumbers, red onion, fresh parsley, and crumbled feta cheese.
4. Drizzle with tzatziki sauce, if desired.
5. Fold in the sides of the wrap and roll it tightly to secure the ingredients inside.
6. Cut the wraps in half, if desired, and serve.

Nutritional Information per Serving:

- Calories: 350
- Proteins: 12g
- Fats: 8g
- Carbs: 58g
- Fiber: 8g
- Sugar: 4g
- Sodium: 560mg
- Omega 3: 0.2g

Greek Lentil Salad

Servings: 4

Preparation Time: 10 minutes

Ingredients:

- 1 cup cooked lentils
- 1 cup diced cucumbers
- 1 cup cherry tomatoes, halved
- 1/2 cup diced red bell pepper
- 1/2 cup crumbled feta cheese
- 1/4 cup sliced Kalamata olives
- 1/4 cup chopped red onion
- 2 tablespoons Extra Virgin Olive Oil
- 2 tablespoons lemon juice
- 1 teaspoon dried oregano
- Salt and pepper to taste
- Fresh parsley for garnish (optional)

Instructions:

1. In a large mixing bowl, combine the cooked lentils, diced cucumbers, cherry tomatoes, red bell pepper, crumbled feta cheese, sliced Kalamata olives, and chopped red onion.
2. In a small bowl, whisk together the Extra Virgin Olive Oil, lemon juice, dried oregano, salt, and pepper to make the dressing.
3. Pour the dressing over the lentil mixture and toss well to coat all the ingredients.
4. Adjust the seasoning with additional salt and pepper, if desired.
5. Garnish with fresh parsley, if desired, for added freshness and color.
6. Serve chilled and enjoy.

Nutritional Information per Serving:

- Calories: 240
- Proteins: 12g
- Fats: 10g
- Carbs: 28g
- Fiber: 9g
- Sugar: 4g
- Sodium: 480mg
- Omega 3: 0.2g

Stuffed Pita Pockets

Servings: 4

Preparation Time: 15 minutes

Ingredients:

- 4 whole wheat pita pockets
- 1 cup cooked quinoa
- 1 cup diced cucumbers
- 1 cup diced tomatoes
- 1/2 cup sliced Kalamata olives
- 1/4 cup chopped red onion
- 1/4 cup crumbled feta cheese
- 2 tablespoons Extra Virgin Olive Oil
- 2 tablespoons lemon juice
- 1 teaspoon dried oregano
- Salt and pepper to taste
- Fresh parsley for garnish (optional)

Instructions:

1. Cut the whole wheat pita pockets in half to create pockets for stuffing.
2. In a large mixing bowl, combine the cooked quinoa, diced cucumbers, diced tomatoes, sliced Kalamata olives, chopped red onion, crumbled feta cheese, Extra Virgin Olive Oil, lemon juice, dried oregano, salt, and pepper. Toss well to combine all the ingredients.
3. Open each pita pocket and fill it with the quinoa and vegetable mixture. Press gently to pack the filling inside the pockets.
4. Garnish with fresh parsley, if desired, for added freshness and color.
5. Serve immediately.

Nutritional Information per Serving:

- Calories: 320
- Proteins: 10g
- Fats: 10g
- Carbs: 50g
- Fiber: 8g
- Sugar: 3g
- Sodium: 480mg
- Omega 3: 0.2g

Aegean Orzo Salad

Servings: 4

Preparation Time: 15 minutes

Ingredients:

- 1 cup orzo pasta
- 1 cup diced cucumbers
- 1 cup cherry tomatoes, halved
- 1/2 cup diced red bell pepper
- 1/2 cup crumbled feta cheese
- 1/4 cup sliced Kalamata olives
- 1/4 cup chopped red onion
- 2 tablespoons Extra Virgin Olive Oil
- 2 tablespoons lemon juice
- 1 teaspoon dried oregano
- Salt and pepper to taste
- Fresh parsley for garnish (optional)

Instructions:

1. Cook the orzo pasta according to the package instructions. Drain and set aside to cool.
2. In a large mixing bowl, combine the cooked and cooled orzo pasta, diced cucumbers, cherry tomatoes, red bell pepper, crumbled feta cheese, sliced Kalamata olives, and chopped red onion.
3. In a small bowl, whisk together the Extra Virgin Olive Oil, lemon juice, dried oregano, salt, and pepper to make the dressing.
4. Pour the dressing over the orzo mixture and toss well to coat all the ingredients.
5. Adjust the seasoning with additional salt and pepper, if desired.
6. Garnish with fresh parsley, if desired, for added freshness and color.
7. Serve chilled and enjoy.

Nutritional Information per Serving:

- Calories: 290
- Proteins: 8g
- Fats: 10g
- Carbs: 40g
- Fiber: 3g
- Sugar: 3g
- Sodium: 360mg
- Omega 3: 0.1g

Greek Chicken Salad

Servings: 4

Preparation Time: 15 minutes

Ingredients:

- 2 boneless, skinless chicken breasts, cooked and diced
- 4 cups mixed salad greens
- 1 cup cherry tomatoes, halved
- 1/2 cup sliced cucumber
- 1/4 cup sliced Kalamata olives
- 1/4 cup crumbled feta cheese
- 1/4 cup chopped red onion
- 2 tablespoons Extra Virgin Olive Oil
- 2 tablespoons lemon juice
- 1 teaspoon dried oregano
- Salt and pepper to taste
- Fresh parsley for garnish (optional)

Instructions:

1. In a large salad bowl, combine the mixed salad greens, cherry tomatoes, sliced cucumber, Kalamata olives, crumbled feta cheese, and chopped red onion.
2. Add the cooked and diced chicken breast to the salad bowl.
3. In a small bowl, whisk together the Extra Virgin Olive Oil, lemon juice, dried oregano, salt, and pepper to make the dressing.
4. Pour the dressing over the salad and toss well to coat all the ingredients.
5. Adjust the seasoning with additional salt and pepper, if desired.
6. Garnish with fresh parsley, if desired, for added freshness and color.
7. Serve immediately and enjoy.

Nutritional Information per Serving:

- Calories: 260
- Proteins: 24g
- Fats: 13g
- Carbs: 10g
- Fiber: 3g
- Sugar: 4g
- Sodium: 380mg
- Omega 3: 0.2g

Southern Veggie Wrap

Servings: 4

Preparation Time: 15 minutes

Ingredients:

- 4 large whole wheat or spinach wraps
- 1 cup hummus
- 1 cup mixed salad greens
- 1/2 cup sliced cucumber
- 1/2 cup sliced bell peppers
- 1/4 cup sliced red onion
- 1/4 cup sliced Kalamata olives
- 1/4 cup crumbled feta cheese
- 2 tablespoons Extra Virgin Olive Oil
- 2 tablespoons lemon juice
- 1 teaspoon dried oregano
- Salt and pepper to taste

Instructions:

1. Lay out the whole wheat or spinach wraps on a clean surface.
2. Spread a generous layer of hummus onto each wrap.
3. In a small bowl, whisk together the Extra Virgin Olive Oil, lemon juice, dried oregano, salt, and pepper to make a dressing.
4. In a separate bowl, combine the mixed salad greens, sliced cucumber, sliced bell peppers, sliced red onion, Kalamata olives, and crumbled feta cheese. Drizzle the dressing over the salad and toss to coat.
5. Divide the salad mixture evenly among the wraps, placing it on one side of each wrap.
6. Roll up the wraps tightly, folding in the sides as you go.
7. Cut each wrap in half and secure with toothpicks, if desired.
8. Serve immediately and enjoy.

Nutritional Information per Serving:

- Calories: 320
- Proteins: 10g
- Fats: 15g
- Carbs: 35g
- Fiber: 8g
- Sugar: 3g
- Sodium: 480mg
- Omega 3: 0.1g

Mediterranean Tuna Salad

Servings: 4

Preparation Time: 10 minutes

Ingredients:

- 2 cans (5 ounces each) tuna, drained
- 1 cup diced cucumber
- 1/2 cup diced tomatoes
- 1/4 cup sliced Kalamata olives
- 1/4 cup crumbled feta cheese
- 2 tablespoons chopped red onion
- 2 tablespoons Extra Virgin Olive Oil
- 2 tablespoons lemon juice
- 1 teaspoon dried oregano
- Salt and pepper to taste
- Fresh parsley for garnish (optional)

Instructions:

1. In a large mixing bowl, combine the drained tuna, diced cucumber, diced tomatoes, Kalamata olives, crumbled feta cheese, and chopped red onion.
2. In a small bowl, whisk together the Extra Virgin Olive Oil, lemon juice, dried oregano, salt, and pepper to make a dressing.
3. Pour the dressing over the tuna mixture and toss gently to coat all the ingredients.
4. Adjust the seasoning with additional salt and pepper, if desired.
5. Garnish with fresh parsley, if desired, for added freshness and flavor.
6. Serve the Mediterranean Tuna Salad on a bed of mixed greens, as a filling for pita pockets, or as a topping for whole grain bread.
7. Enjoy this protein-packed and flavorful salad!

Nutritional Information per Serving:

- Calories: 210
- Proteins: 22g
- Fats: 12g
- Carbs: 4g
- Fiber: 1g
- Sugar: 1g
- Sodium: 480mg
- Omega 3: 0.6g

Quinoa Salad

Servings: 4

Preparation Time: 15 minutes

Ingredients:

- 1 cup cooked quinoa
- 1 cup diced cucumber
- 1 cup diced tomatoes
- 1/2 cup diced red bell pepper
- 1/4 cup sliced Kalamata olives
- 1/4 cup crumbled feta cheese
- 2 tablespoons chopped red onion
- 2 tablespoons Extra Virgin Olive Oil
- 2 tablespoons lemon juice
- 1 teaspoon dried oregano
- Salt and pepper to taste
- Fresh parsley for garnish (optional)

Instructions:

1. In a large mixing bowl, combine the cooked quinoa, diced cucumber, diced tomatoes, diced red bell pepper, Kalamata olives, crumbled feta cheese, and chopped red onion.
2. In a small bowl, whisk together the Extra Virgin Olive Oil, lemon juice, dried oregano, salt, and pepper to make a dressing.
3. Pour the dressing over the quinoa mixture and toss gently to coat all the ingredients.
4. Adjust the seasoning with additional salt and pepper, if desired.
5. Garnish with fresh parsley, if desired, for added freshness and flavor.
6. Serve the Mediterranean Quinoa Salad as a refreshing and satisfying side dish or as a light lunch.
7. Enjoy the vibrant flavors and textures of this Mediterranean-inspired quinoa salad!

Nutritional Information per Serving:

- Calories: 220
- Proteins: 7g
- Fats: 10g
- Carbs: 26g
- Fiber: 4g
- Sugar: 3g
- Sodium: 320mg
- Omega 3: 0.2g

Greek Salad with Grilled Chicken

Servings: 4

Preparation Time: 15 minutes

Cooking Time: 12 minutes

Ingredients:

- 2 boneless, skinless chicken breasts
- 4 cups mixed salad greens
- 1 cup cherry tomatoes, halved
- 1/2 cup sliced cucumber
- 1/4 cup sliced red onion
- 1/4 cup sliced Kalamata olives
- 1/4 cup crumbled feta cheese
- 2 tablespoons Extra Virgin Olive Oil
- 2 tablespoons lemon juice
- 1 teaspoon dried oregano
- Salt and pepper to taste

Instructions:

1. Preheat the grill to medium-high heat.
2. Season the chicken breasts with salt, pepper, and dried oregano.
3. Grill the chicken breasts for about 6 minutes per side or until cooked through. Allow the chicken to rest for a few minutes before slicing it into strips.
4. In a large salad bowl, combine the mixed salad greens, cherry tomatoes, sliced cucumber, sliced red onion, Kalamata olives, and crumbled feta cheese.
5. In a small bowl, whisk together the Extra Virgin Olive Oil and lemon juice to make a dressing. Season with salt, pepper, and dried oregano.
6. Pour the dressing over the salad and toss gently to coat all the ingredients.
7. Divide the salad among serving plates and top with the grilled chicken strips.
8. Serve the Greek Salad with Grilled Chicken as a satisfying and flavorful meal.

Nutritional Information per Serving:

- Calories: 230
- Proteins: 26g
- Fats: 11g
- Carbs: 8g

- Fiber: 2g
- Sugar: 4g
- Sodium: 360mg
- Omega 3: 0.3g

Couscous Mixed Salad

Servings: 4

Preparation Time: 15 minutes

Cooking Time: 5 minutes

Ingredients:

- 1 cup couscous
- 1 ¼ cups vegetable broth
- 1 cup cherry tomatoes, halved
- 1 cucumber, diced
- ½ red onion, thinly sliced
- ½ cup Kalamata olives, pitted and halved
- ¼ cup crumbled feta cheese
- 2 tablespoons chopped fresh parsley
- 2 tablespoons Extra Virgin Olive Oil
- 1 tablespoon lemon juice
- 1 teaspoon dried oregano
- Salt and pepper to taste

Instructions:

1. In a medium saucepan, bring the vegetable broth to a boil. Add the couscous, cover, and remove from heat. Let it sit for 5 minutes or until the liquid is absorbed. Fluff the couscous with a fork.
2. In a large salad bowl, combine the cooked couscous, cherry tomatoes, diced cucumber, sliced red onion, Kalamata olives, crumbled feta cheese, and chopped fresh parsley.
3. In a small bowl, whisk together the Extra Virgin Olive Oil, lemon juice, dried oregano, salt, and pepper to make a dressing.
4. Pour the dressing over the couscous salad and toss gently to combine all the ingredients and coat them evenly.
5. Taste and adjust the seasoning if needed.
6. Serve the Mediterranean Couscous Salad as a refreshing and satisfying side dish or light meal.

Nutritional Information per Serving:

- Calories: 280
- Proteins: 7g
- Fats: 9g
- Carbs: 43g
- Fiber: 4g
- Sugar: 4g
- Sodium: 570mg
- Omega 3: 0.2g

Greek Veggie Wrap

Servings: 2

Preparation Time: 10 minutes

Ingredients:

- 2 whole wheat tortilla wraps
- ½ cup hummus
- 1 cup mixed salad greens
- ½ cup cherry tomatoes, halved
- ½ cucumber, thinly sliced
- ½ red onion, thinly sliced
- ¼ cup Kalamata olives, pitted and sliced
- 2 tablespoons crumbled feta cheese
- 2 tablespoons Greek salad dressing

Instructions:

1. Lay the tortilla wraps flat on a clean surface.
2. Spread ¼ cup of hummus evenly on each tortilla.

3. Place a handful of mixed salad greens in the center of each wrap.

4. Top with cherry tomatoes, cucumber slices, red onion slices, Kalamata olives, and crumbled feta cheese.

5. Drizzle 1 tablespoon of Greek salad dressing over each wrap.

6. Fold in the sides of the tortilla, then roll it up tightly from bottom to top to create a wrap.

7. Slice the wraps in half diagonally, if desired.

8. Serve the Greek Veggie Wraps as a delicious and nutritious lunch or light dinner option.

Nutritional Information per Serving:

- Calories: 330
- Proteins: 9g
- Fats: 14g
- Carbs: 40g
- Fiber: 8g
- Sugar: 4g
- Sodium: 620mg
- Omega 3: 0.2g

We hope this chapter has inspired you to create flavorful and satisfying lunches that can be enjoyed wherever you are. Remember, with a little planning and the right recipes, you can nourish your body and energize your day even on the busiest of schedules.

Feel free to mix and match these recipes, adapt them to your taste preferences, and get creative with your own variations. Don't forget to refer back to the nutritional information per serving provided for each recipe to help you make informed choices about your meals.

Chapter 6. Effortless Low-Carb Dinners

A collection of delicious low-carb recipes that are designed to make your dinner preparations a breeze. After a long day, the last thing you want is a complicated and time-consuming meal. That's why we have curated a selection of recipes that are not only easy to make but also packed with flavor and wholesome ingredients.

From quick and satisfying weeknight meals to dishes that can impress your guests, we have you covered. Each recipe is crafted with simplicity in mind, using readily available ingredients to create dishes that will tantalize your taste buds and leave you feeling satisfied.

So, get ready to indulge in effortless dinners that will nourish your body and delight your senses.

Keto Cauliflower Mac and Cheese

Servings: 4

Preparation Time: 15 minutes
Cooking Time: 20 minutes

Ingredients:

- Cauliflower: 1 medium head, cut into florets
- Heavy cream: 1 cup (240ml)
- Cream cheese: 4 ounces (113g), softened
- Cheddar cheese: 1 ½ cups (170g), shredded
- Garlic powder: 1 teaspoon
- Onion powder: 1 teaspoon
- Salt and pepper to taste
- Fresh parsley (optional): for garnish

Instructions:

1.   Preheat the oven to 375°F (190°C) and lightly grease a baking dish.
2.   Bring a large pot of water to a boil. Add the cauliflower florets and cook for 5-7 minutes, until tender but still slightly firm. Drain well and set aside.
3.   In a saucepan, heat the heavy cream over medium heat until hot but not boiling.
4.   Add the cream cheese, cheddar cheese, garlic powder, onion powder, salt, and pepper to the saucepan. Stir until the cheeses have melted and the mixture is smooth.
5.   Add the cooked cauliflower to the cheese sauce, stirring gently to coat the florets evenly.
6.   Transfer the cauliflower mixture to the prepared baking dish and spread it out evenly.
7.   Bake in the preheated oven for 15-20 minutes, until the top is golden and bubbly.
8.   Garnish with fresh parsley if desired, then serve hot.

Nutritional Information per Serving:

- Calories: 250
- Proteins:10g
- Fats:20g
- Carbs:6g
- Fiber:2g
- Sugar:3g
- Sodium:380mg
- Omega 3:0.2g

Buffalo Chicken Lettuce Wraps

Servings: 4

Preparation Time: 15 minutes
Cooking Time: 15 minutes

Ingredients:

- Chicken breasts: 2, boneless, skinless
- Buffalo sauce: ½ cup (120ml)
- Ranch dressing: ¼ cup (60ml)
- Lettuce leaves (such as iceberg or butter lettuce): 8-10 leaves
- Celery: 2 stalks, finely chopped
- Carrots: 2 medium, grated
- Blue cheese crumbles: ¼ cup (30g), for topping (optional)
- Green onions: 2, sliced (for garnish)

Instructions:

1.   Preheat a grill or grill pan to medium-high heat.
2.   Season the chicken breasts with salt and pepper. Grill the chicken for 6-8 minutes per side, or until cooked through.
3.   Remove the chicken from the grill and let it rest for a few minutes. Then, shred the chicken using two forks.
4.   In a mixing bowl, combine the shredded chicken with the buffalo sauce and ranch dressing. Mix well to coat the chicken evenly.
5.   Take a lettuce leaf and spoon some of the buffalo chicken mixture onto it.
6.   Top with chopped celery, grated carrots, and blue cheese crumbles (if desired).
7.   Garnish with sliced green onions.
8.   Repeat with the remaining lettuce leaves and buffalo chicken mixture.

9.   Serve the buffalo chicken lettuce wraps as a delicious low carb meal.

Nutritional Information per Serving:

- Calories: 220
- Proteins: 30g
- Fats: 7g
- Carbs: 4g
- Fiber: 1g
- Sugar: 2g
- Sodium: 950mg
- Omega 3: 0.3g

Beef and Broccoli Stir-Fry

Servings: 4

Preparation Time: 15 minutes
Cooking Time: 10 minutes

Ingredients:

- Beef sirloin or flank steak: 1 pound (450g), thinly sliced
- Broccoli florets: 3 cups (300g)
- Soy sauce: ⅓ cup (80ml), low sodium
- Beef broth: ¼ cup (60ml)
- Garlic: 3 cloves, minced
- Ginger: 1 tablespoon, grated
- Sesame oil: 2 tablespoons
- Olive oil: 1 tablespoon
- Red pepper flakes (optional): to taste
- Sesame seeds: 1 tablespoon (for garnish)
- Green onions: 2, sliced (for garnish)

Instructions:

1.   In a small bowl, whisk together the soy sauce, beef broth, minced garlic, grated ginger, and red pepper flakes (if using). Set aside.
2.   Heat the olive oil in a large skillet or wok over high heat.

3.   Add the sliced beef to the skillet and cook for 2-3 minutes, until browned. Remove the beef from the skillet and set aside.
4.   n the same skillet, add the broccoli florets and stir-fry for 3-4 minutes, until crisp-tender.
5.   Return the beef to the skillet with the broccoli.
6.   Pour the soy sauce mixture over the beef and broccoli. Stir-fry for an additional 2-3 minutes, until the sauce thickens and coats the beef and broccoli.
7.   Drizzle the sesame oil over the stir-fry and toss to combine.
8.   Garnish with sesame seeds and sliced green onions.
9.   Serve the beef and broccoli stir-fry hot over steamed cauliflower rice or with low carb noodles.

Nutritional Information per Serving:

- Calories: 280
- Proteins: 30g
- Fats: 14g
- Carbs: 8g
- Fiber: 3g
- Sugar: 2g
- Sodium: 800mg
- Omega 3: 0.5g

Zucchini Noodle Carbonara

Servings: 4

Preparation Time: 15 minutes
Cooking Time: 10 minutes

Ingredients:

- Zucchini: 4 medium-sized
- Bacon: 6 slices, chopped
- Eggs: 2
- Parmesan cheese: ½ cup (50g), grated
- Garlic: 2 cloves, minced
- Black pepper: ½ teaspoon
- Olive oil: 1 tablespoon
- Fresh parsley (optional): for garnish

Instructions:

1.   Using a spiralizer or julienne peeler, turn the zucchini into noodle-like strands. Set aside.
2.   In a large skillet, cook the chopped bacon over medium heat until crispy. Remove the bacon from the skillet, leaving the drippings.
3.   In a bowl, whisk together the eggs, grated Parmesan cheese, minced garlic, and black pepper.
4.   Heat the olive oil in the skillet with the bacon drippings over medium heat.
5.   Add the zucchini noodles to the skillet and sauté for 2-3 minutes, until slightly softened.
6.   Reduce the heat to low and pour the egg mixture over the zucchini noodles. Quickly toss the noodles to coat them evenly with the egg mixture.
7.   Continue to cook for 2-3 minutes, stirring constantly, until the eggs are cooked and form a creamy sauce.
8.   Remove the skillet from heat and stir in the crispy bacon.
9.   Garnish with fresh parsley if desired, then serve the zucchini noodle carbonara immediately.

Nutritional Information per Serving:

- Calories: 210
- Proteins: 15g
- Fats : 14g
- Carbs: 9g
- Fiber: 3g
- Sugar: 4g
- Sodium: 480mg
- Omega 3: 0.2g

Baked Lemon Herb Chicken Thighs

Servings: 4

Preparation Time: 10 minutes
Cooking Time: 35-40 minutes

Ingredients:

- Chicken thighs: 4, bone-in, skin-on
- Lemon: 1, juiced and zested
- Garlic: 4 cloves, minced
- Fresh thyme: 1 tablespoon, chopped
- Fresh rosemary: 1 tablespoon, chopped
- Extra Virgin Olive Oil: 2 tablespoons
- Salt and pepper to taste

Instructions:

1.   Preheat the oven to 400°F (200°C) and line a baking sheet with foil.
2.   In a small bowl, combine the lemon juice, lemon zest, minced garlic, chopped thyme, chopped rosemary, Extra Virgin Olive Oil, salt, and pepper. Mix well.
3.   Place the chicken thighs on the prepared baking sheet.
4.   Brush the lemon herb mixture over the chicken thighs, ensuring they are well coated.
5.   Bake in the preheated oven for 35-40 minutes, or until the chicken thighs are cooked through and the skin is crispy and golden.
6.   Remove from the oven and let the chicken thighs rest for a few minutes before serving.
7.   Serve the baked lemon herb chicken thighs with your choice of low carb side

dishes, such as roasted vegetables or a fresh salad.

Nutritional Information per Serving:

- Calories: 280
- Proteins: 25g
- Fats: 19g
- Carbs: 2g
- Fiber: -
- Sugar: -
- Sodium: 340mg
- Omega 3: 0.2g

Spinach and Feta Stuffed Chicken Breast

Servings: 4

Preparation Time: 15 minutes
Cooking Time: 25-30 minutes

Ingredients:

- Chicken breasts: 4, boneless, skinless
- Spinach: 2 cups (60g), fresh or frozen
- Feta cheese: ½ cup (75g), crumbled
- Garlic: 2 cloves, minced
- Extra Virgin Olive Oil: 2 tablespoons
- Salt and pepper to taste
- Toothpicks

Instructions:

1. Preheat the oven to 400°F (200°C) and line a baking dish with foil.
2. If using frozen spinach, thaw and squeeze out excess moisture. If using fresh spinach, blanch and squeeze out excess moisture.
3. In a mixing bowl, combine the spinach, feta cheese, minced garlic, salt, and pepper. Mix well.
4. Use a sharp knife to create a pocket in each chicken breast by making a horizontal slit along one side, being careful not to cut all the way through.
5. Stuff each chicken breast with the spinach and feta mixture, pressing it in and closing the pocket. Secure with toothpicks if needed.
6. Heat Extra Virgin Olive Oil in a large skillet over medium-high heat. Sear the stuffed chicken breasts for 2-3 minutes on each side until golden brown.
7. Transfer the seared chicken breasts to the prepared baking dish.
8. Bake in the preheated oven for 20-25 minutes, or until the chicken is cooked through and no longer pink in the center.
9. Remove the toothpicks before serving.
10. Serve the spinach and feta stuffed chicken breast with your choice of low carb sides, such as roasted vegetables or cauliflower rice.

Nutritional Information per Serving:

- Calories: 320
- Proteins: 40g
- Fats: 14g
- Carbs: 2g
- Fiber: 1g
- Sugar: -
- Sodium: 450mg
- Omega 3: 0.3g

BBQ Bacon-Wrapped Shrimp Skewers

Servings: 4

Preparation Time: 15 minutes
Cooking Time: 10 minutes

Ingredients:

- Shrimp: 1 pound (450g), peeled and deveined
- Bacon slices: 8, cut in half
- BBQ sauce: ¼ cup (60ml)
- Smoked paprika: 1 teaspoon
- Garlic powder: 1 teaspoon
- Wooden skewers (pre-soaked in water): 8-10
- Fresh parsley (optional): for garnish

Instructions:

1. Preheat the grill to medium-high heat.
2. In a small bowl, whisk together the BBQ sauce, smoked paprika, and garlic powder.
3. Wrap each shrimp with a half slice of bacon and thread onto the wooden skewers, alternating shrimp and bacon.
4. Brush the BBQ sauce mixture onto the bacon-wrapped shrimp skewers, ensuring they are well coated.
5. Place the skewers on the preheated grill and cook for 3-4 minutes per side, or until the shrimp is pink and cooked through, and the bacon is crispy.
6. Remove the skewers from the grill and let them rest for a few minutes.
7. Garnish with fresh parsley if desired, then serve the BBQ bacon-wrapped shrimp skewers as a delicious low carb appetizer or main dish.

Nutritional Information per Serving:

- Calories: 220
- Proteins: 25g
- Fats: 11g
- Carbs: 6g
- Fiber: -
- Sugar: 5g
- Sodium: 520mg
- Omega 3: 0.3g

Low Carb Shepherd's Pie

Servings: 6

Preparation Time: 15 minutes
Cooking Time: 45 minutes

Ingredients:

- Cauliflower: 1 medium head, cut into florets
- Ground beef: 1 pound (450g)
- Onion: 1 medium, chopped
- Garlic: 2 cloves, minced
- Tomato paste: 2 tablespoons
- Worcestershire sauce: 1 tablespoon
- Beef broth: ½ cup (120ml)
- Frozen mixed vegetables: 1 cup (150g)
- Salt and pepper to taste
- Butter: 2 tablespoons
- Heavy cream: ¼ cup (60ml)
- Shredded cheddar cheese: 1 cup (115g), divided
- Fresh parsley (optional): for garnish

Instructions:

1. Preheat the oven to 375°F (190°C).
2. Steam the cauliflower florets until tender. Drain well and transfer to a large bowl.
3. In a large skillet, brown the ground beef over medium heat until fully cooked. Drain excess fat if needed.
4. Add the chopped onion and minced garlic to the skillet with the ground beef. Sauté until the onion is translucent.
5. Stir in the tomato paste, Worcestershire sauce, and beef broth. Mix well to combine.
6. Add the frozen mixed vegetables to the skillet and cook for a few minutes until heated through.
7. Season with salt and pepper to taste.
8. Meanwhile, mash the steamed cauliflower with butter and heavy cream until smooth and creamy. Season with salt and pepper.
9. Transfer the ground beef mixture to a baking dish. Spread the mashed cauliflower evenly over the top.
10. Sprinkle half of the shredded cheddar cheese over the cauliflower layer.

11. Bake in the preheated oven for 20-25 minutes, or until the cheese is melted and bubbly.
12. Remove from the oven and sprinkle the remaining shredded cheddar cheese over the top. Return to the oven and bake for an additional 5 minutes until the cheese is golden and melted.
13. Garnish with fresh parsley if desired, then serve the low carb Shepherd's Pie hot.

Nutritional Information per Serving:

- Calories: 340
- Proteins: 25g
- Fats: 22g
- Carbs: 11g
- Fiber: 4g
- Sugar: 4g
- Sodium: 520mg
- Omega 3: 0.2g

Creamy Garlic Parmesan Salmon

Servings: 4

Preparation Time: 10 minutes
Cooking Time: 15 minutes

Ingredients:

- Salmon fillets: 4, skin-on
- Garlic: 3 cloves, minced
- Parmesan cheese: ½ cup (50g), grated
- Heavy cream: ½ cup (120ml)
- Butter: 2 tablespoons
- Lemon juice: 2 tablespoons
- Fresh parsley: 2 tablespoons, chopped
- Salt and pepper to taste

Instructions:

1. Preheat the oven to 400°F (200°C) and line a baking sheet with foil.
2. Season the salmon fillets with salt and pepper. Place them on the prepared baking sheet, skin-side down.
3. In a small saucepan, melt the butter over medium heat. Add the minced garlic and sauté until fragrant.
4. Add the heavy cream and grated Parmesan cheese to the saucepan. Stir well and cook until the cheese is melted and the sauce thickens.
5. Remove the saucepan from heat and stir in the lemon juice and chopped parsley.
6. Spoon the creamy garlic Parmesan sauce over the salmon fillets, ensuring they are well coated.
7. Bake in the preheated oven for 12-15 minutes, or until the salmon is cooked through and flakes easily with a fork.
8. Remove from the oven and let the salmon rest for a few minutes before serving.
9. Serve the creamy garlic Parmesan salmon hot, garnished with additional chopped parsley.

Nutritional Information per Serving:

- Calories: 350
- Proteins: 30g

- Fats: 24g
- Carbs: 2g
- Fiber: -
- Sugar: -
- Sodium: 400mg
- Omega 3: 0.8g

Turkey Taco Lettuce Wraps

Servings: 4

Preparation Time: 10 minutes
Cooking Time: 15 minutes

Ingredients:

- Ground turkey: 1 pound (450g)
- Onion: 1 medium, chopped
- Garlic: 2 cloves, minced
- Taco seasoning: 2 tablespoons
- Tomato: 1 medium, diced
- Bell pepper: 1 medium, diced
- Black beans: ½ cup (90g), drained and rinsed
- Lettuce leaves (such as iceberg or butter lettuce): 8-10 leaves
- Avocado: 1, diced
- Greek yogurt (optional): for topping
- Fresh cilantro (optional): for garnish

Instructions:

1. In a large skillet, cook the ground turkey over medium heat until browned and cooked through. Break it up into crumbles using a spatula.
2. Add the chopped onion and minced garlic to the skillet with the ground turkey. Sauté until the onion is translucent.
3. Stir in the taco seasoning and cook for another minute to allow the flavors to meld.
4. Add the diced tomato, diced bell pepper, and black beans to the skillet. Stir well and cook for a few minutes until heated through.
5. Wash and dry the lettuce leaves. Place them on a platter or individual plates.
6. Spoon the turkey taco mixture onto each lettuce leaf, distributing it evenly.

7. Top with diced avocado and a dollop of Greek yogurt if desired.
8. Garnish with fresh cilantro if desired.
9. Serve the turkey taco lettuce wraps as a tasty and low carb alternative to traditional tacos.

Nutritional Information per Serving:

- Calories: 260
- Proteins: 25g
- Fats: 12g
- Carbs: 15g
- Fiber: 5g
- Sugar: 3g
- Sodium: 430mg
- Omega 3: 0.4g

Greek Lemon Chicken with Cauliflower Rice

Servings: 4

Preparation Time: 15 minutes
Cooking Time: 20 minutes

Ingredients:

- Chicken breasts: 4, boneless, skinless
- Lemon: 1, juiced and zested
- Garlic: 3 cloves, minced
- Greek seasoning: 1 tablespoon
- Extra Virgin Olive Oil: 2 tablespoons
- Cauliflower: 1 medium head, grated or processed into rice-like texture
- Cherry tomatoes: 1 cup (150g), halved
- Kalamata olives: ½ cup (75g), pitted and sliced
- Fresh parsley: 2 tablespoons, chopped
- Salt and pepper to taste

Instructions:

1. Preheat the oven to 400°F (200°C) and line a baking dish with foil.
2. Place the chicken breasts in the baking dish.

3. In a small bowl, combine the lemon juice, lemon zest, minced garlic, Greek seasoning, Extra Virgin Olive Oil, salt, and pepper. Mix well.
4. Pour the lemon garlic marinade over the chicken breasts, ensuring they are well coated. Let marinate for at least 15 minutes.
5. Bake the chicken in the preheated oven for 15-20 minutes, or until cooked through and no longer pink in the center.
6. While the chicken is baking, prepare the cauliflower rice. Grate or process the cauliflower into a rice-like texture.
7. Heat a tablespoon of Extra Virgin Olive Oil in a large skillet over medium heat. Add the cauliflower rice and sauté for 5-6 minutes until tender.
8. Stir in the halved cherry tomatoes and sliced Kalamata olives. Cook for an additional 2-3 minutes.
9. Season the cauliflower rice mixture with salt and pepper to taste.
10. Remove the chicken from the oven and let it rest for a few minutes. Slice the chicken into strips.
11. Serve the Greek lemon chicken over a bed of cauliflower rice. Garnish with fresh parsley.

Nutritional Information per Serving:

- Calories: 280
- Proteins: 35g
- Fats: 10g
- Carbs: 12g
- Fiber: 5g
- Sugar: 3g
- Sodium: 490mg
- Omega 3: 0.4g

Grilled Mediterranean Vegetables with Feta

Servings: 4

Preparation Time: 15 minutes
Grilling Time: 10-15 minutes

Ingredients:

- Zucchini: 2 medium-sized, sliced lengthwise
- Eggplant: 1 medium-sized, sliced lengthwise
- Bell peppers: 2, sliced into strips
- Red onion: 1, sliced into rings
- Cherry tomatoes: 1 cup (150g), halved
- Extra Virgin Olive Oil: 2 tablespoons
- Balsamic vinegar: 2 tablespoons
- Garlic: 3 cloves, minced
- Fresh basil: 2 tablespoons, chopped
- Salt and pepper to taste
- Feta cheese: ½ cup (75g), crumbled

Instructions:

1. Preheat the grill to medium-high heat.
2. In a large bowl, combine the sliced zucchini, eggplant, bell peppers, red onion, and cherry tomatoes.
3. In a small bowl, whisk together the Extra Virgin Olive Oil, balsamic vinegar, minced garlic, chopped basil, salt, and pepper to make the marinade.
4. Pour the marinade over the vegetables and toss to coat them evenly.
5. Place the vegetables on the preheated grill and cook for 5-7 minutes per side, or until they are tender and grill marks appear.
6. Remove the grilled vegetables from the heat and let them cool slightly.
7. Cut the grilled vegetables into bite-sized pieces and transfer them to a serving platter.
8. Sprinkle the crumbled feta cheese over the grilled vegetables.
9. Serve the grilled Mediterranean vegetables with feta as a delicious side dish or as a light main course.

Nutritional Information per Serving:

- Calories: 180
- Proteins: 6g
- Fats: 12g
- Carbs: 15g
- Fiber: 6g
- Sugar: 8g
- Sodium: 350mg
- Omega 3: 0.2g

Italian Stuffed Bell Peppers

Servings: 4

Preparation Time: 15 minutes
Cooking Time: 35-40 minutes

Ingredients:

- Bell peppers: 4, any color
- Ground beef: 1 pound (450g)
- Onion: 1 medium, chopped
- Garlic: 2 cloves, minced
- Tomato sauce: 1 cup (240ml)
- Italian seasoning: 1 tablespoon
- Mozzarella cheese: ½ cup (60g), shredded
- Parmesan cheese: ¼ cup (25g), grated
- Fresh basil: 2 tablespoons, chopped
- Salt and pepper to taste

Instructions:

1. Preheat the oven to 375°F (190°C) and line a baking dish with foil.
2. Cut the tops off the bell peppers and remove the seeds and membranes. Set aside.

3. In a large skillet, cook the ground beef over medium heat until browned and cooked through. Drain excess fat if needed.
4. Add the chopped onion and minced garlic to the skillet with the ground beef. Sauté until the onion is translucent.
5. Stir in the tomato sauce and Italian seasoning. Cook for another minute to allow the flavors to meld. Season with salt and pepper to taste.
6. Spoon the ground beef mixture into the hollowed-out bell peppers, filling them to the top.
7. Place the stuffed bell peppers in the prepared baking dish.
8. Sprinkle the shredded mozzarella cheese and grated Parmesan cheese over the top of each bell pepper.
9. Bake in the preheated oven for 30-35 minutes, or until the bell peppers are tender and the cheese is melted and golden.
10. Remove from the oven and let the stuffed bell peppers cool for a few minutes.
11. Garnish with fresh chopped basil before serving.

Nutritional Information per Serving:

- Calories: 290
- Proteins: 25g
- Fats: 16g
- Carbs: 10g
- Fiber: 2g
- Sugar: 5g
- Sodium: 520mg
- Omega 3: 0.2g

Spanish Garlic Shrimp (Gambas al Ajillo)

Servings: 4

Preparation Time: 10 minutes
Cooking Time: 5-7 minutes

Ingredients:

- Shrimp: 1 pound (450g), peeled and deveined
- Garlic: 6 cloves, thinly sliced
- Extra Virgin Olive Oil: ¼ cup (60ml)
- Red pepper flakes: ½ teaspoon (adjust to taste)
- Smoked paprika: 1 teaspoon
- Lemon: 1, juiced
- Fresh parsley: 2 tablespoons, chopped
- Salt to taste

Instructions:

1. Heat Extra Virgin Olive Oil in a large skillet over medium heat.
2. Add the thinly sliced garlic to the skillet and cook until fragrant and lightly golden.
3. Add the red pepper flakes and smoked paprika to the skillet and stir briefly.
4. Add the shrimp to the skillet and cook for 2-3 minutes per side, or until they turn pink and are cooked through.
5. Squeeze the juice of the lemon over the shrimp and sprinkle with fresh chopped parsley.
6. Season with salt to taste and give everything a quick stir.
7. Remove from heat and transfer the Spanish garlic shrimp to a serving platter.
8. Serve the Gambas al Ajillo hot as a delicious appetizer or with a side of cauliflower rice or crusty bread.

Nutritional Information per Serving:

- Calories: 180
- Proteins: 25g
- Fats: 8g
- Carbs: 2g
- Fiber: -
- Sugar: -
- Sodium: 400mg
- Omega 3: 0.3

Moroccan Spiced Salmon with Roasted Vegetables

Servings: 4

Preparation Time: 15 minutes
Cooking Time: 20-25 minutes

Ingredients:

- Salmon fillets: 4, skin-on
- Carrots: 2 large, peeled and sliced
- Zucchini: 2 medium-sized, sliced
- Red bell pepper: 1, sliced
- Red onion: 1, sliced
- Extra Virgin Olive Oil: 3 tablespoons
- Moroccan spice blend: 1 tablespoon
- Salt and pepper to taste
- Lemon wedges: for serving
- Fresh cilantro or parsley: for garnish

Instructions:

1. Preheat the oven to 400°F (200°C) and line a baking sheet with foil.
2. Place the salmon fillets on one side of the prepared baking sheet.
3. In a large bowl, combine the sliced carrots, zucchini, red bell pepper, and red onion.
4. Drizzle the vegetables with Extra Virgin Olive Oil and sprinkle with the Moroccan spice blend. Toss to coat them evenly.
5. Spread the seasoned vegetables on the other side of the baking sheet, keeping them separate from the salmon.
6. Season the salmon fillets with salt and pepper to taste.
7. Roast in the preheated oven for 20-25 minutes, or until the salmon is cooked through and flakes easily with a fork, and the vegetables are tender.
8. Remove from the oven and let it cool for a few minutes.
9. Serve the Moroccan spiced salmon alongside the roasted vegetables.
10. Squeeze fresh lemon juice over the salmon fillets and garnish with fresh cilantro or parsley.
11. Serve with additional lemon wedges on the side.

Nutritional Information per Serving:

- Calories: 320
- Proteins: 30g
- Fats: 18g
- Carbs: 12g
- Fiber: 5g
- Sugar: 6g
- Sodium: 420mg
- Omega 3: 0.9g

Greek Lamb Meatballs with Tzatziki Sauce

Servings: 4

Preparation Time: 15 minutes
Cooking Time: 15 minutes

Ingredients:

For the Lamb Meatballs:

- Ground lamb: 1 pound (450g)
- Onion: 1 small, finely chopped
- Garlic: 3 cloves, minced
- Fresh parsley: ¼ cup (15g), chopped
- Fresh mint: 2 tablespoons, chopped
- Ground cumin: 1 teaspoon
- Ground coriander: 1 teaspoon
- Salt and pepper to taste
- Extra Virgin Olive Oil: 2 tablespoons (for cooking)

For the Tzatziki Sauce:

- Greek yogurt: 1 cup (240g)
- Cucumber: ½, grated and squeezed to remove excess moisture
- Garlic: 1 clove, minced
- Lemon juice: 1 tablespoon
- Fresh dill: 1 tablespoon, chopped
- Salt and pepper to taste

Instructions:

1. In a large mixing bowl, combine the ground lamb, finely chopped onion, minced garlic, chopped parsley, chopped

mint, ground cumin, ground coriander, salt, and pepper. Mix well until all the ingredients are evenly incorporated.

2. Shape the mixture into small meatballs, about 1-2 tablespoons each.
3. Heat Extra Virgin Olive Oil in a skillet over medium heat.
4. Add the lamb meatballs to the skillet and cook for 12-15 minutes, turning occasionally, until browned and cooked through.
5. While the meatballs are cooking, prepare the Tzatziki sauce. In a small bowl, combine the Greek yogurt, grated cucumber, minced garlic, lemon juice, chopped dill, salt, and pepper. Stir well to combine.
6. Once the meatballs are cooked, remove them from the skillet and let them rest for a few minutes.
7. Serve the Greek lamb meatballs with the homemade Tzatziki sauce on the side for dipping or drizzling.
8. Enjoy the flavorful Greek-inspired meatballs as a delicious appetizer or as part of a main course.

Nutritional Information per Serving (for the Lamb Meatballs):

- Calories: 350
- Proteins: 25g
- Fats: 26g
- Carbs: 4g
- Fiber: 1g
- Sugar: 1g
- Sodium: 480mg
- Omega 3: 0.3g

Baked Cod with Tomato and Olives

Servings: 4

Preparation Time: 10 minutes
Cooking Time: 20 minutes

Ingredients:

- Cod fillets: 4, skinless
- Cherry tomatoes: 1 cup (150g), halved
- Kalamata olives: ½ cup (75g), pitted and sliced
- Red onion: 1 small, thinly sliced
- Garlic: 3 cloves, minced
- Extra Virgin Olive Oil: 2 tablespoons
- Lemon: 1, juiced
- Fresh parsley: 2 tablespoons, chopped
- Dried oregano: 1 teaspoon
- Salt and pepper to taste

Instructions:

1. Preheat the oven to 400°F (200°C) and line a baking dish with foil.
2. Place the cod fillets in the prepared baking dish.
3. In a bowl, combine the cherry tomatoes, Kalamata olives, thinly sliced red onion, minced garlic, Extra Virgin Olive Oil, lemon juice, chopped parsley, dried oregano, salt, and pepper. Toss to coat the ingredients evenly.
4. Spoon the tomato and olive mixture over the cod fillets, covering them completely.
5. Bake in the preheated oven for 15-20 minutes, or until the cod is cooked through and flakes easily with a fork.
6. Remove from the oven and let it cool for a few minutes.
7. Serve the Mediterranean baked cod hot, garnished with additional chopped parsley.
8. Enjoy this flavorful and healthy seafood dish as a main course.

Nutritional Information per Serving:

- Calories: 220
- Proteins: 30g
- Fats: 10g
- Carbs: 5g
- Fiber: 1g

- Sugar: 2g
- Sodium: 480mg
- Omega 3: 0.3g

Lebanese Chicken Shawarma with Garlic Sauce

Servings: 4

Preparation Time: 15 minutes (+ marinating time)
Cooking Time: 15 minutes

Ingredients:

For the Chicken Shawarma:
- Chicken breasts: 2, boneless and skinless
- Lemon juice: ¼ cup (60ml)
- Extra Virgin Olive Oil: 2 tablespoons
- Garlic: 3 cloves, minced
- Ground cumin: 1 teaspoon
- Ground coriander: 1 teaspoon
- Paprika: 1 teaspoon
- Ground turmeric: ½ teaspoon
- Ground cinnamon: ½ teaspoon
- Salt and pepper to taste

For the Garlic Sauce:
- Greek yogurt: ½ cup (120g)
- Garlic: 3 cloves, minced
- Lemon juice: 1 tablespoon
- Fresh parsley: 2 tablespoons, chopped
- Salt and pepper to taste

For Serving:
- Pita bread or flatbread
- Sliced tomatoes
- Sliced cucumbers
- Chopped fresh parsley

Instructions:

1. In a bowl, combine the lemon juice, Extra Virgin Olive Oil, minced garlic, ground cumin, ground coriander, paprika, ground turmeric, ground cinnamon, salt, and pepper to make the marinade.
2. Slice the chicken breasts into thin strips and add them to the marinade. Coat the chicken evenly and let it marinate for at least 30 minutes, or overnight for a more intense flavor.
3. While the chicken is marinating, prepare the garlic sauce. In a small bowl, mix together the Greek yogurt, minced garlic, lemon juice, chopped parsley, salt, and pepper. Stir well to combine. Refrigerate until ready to serve.
4. Heat a large skillet or grill pan over medium-high heat. Cook the marinated chicken strips for 5-6 minutes per side, or until cooked through and nicely browned.
5. Remove the chicken from the heat and let it rest for a few minutes.
6. Warm the pita bread or flatbread in a toaster or oven.
7. To assemble the shawarma, spread a generous amount of garlic sauce on the warmed pita bread or flatbread.
8. Add the cooked chicken strips, sliced tomatoes, sliced cucumbers, and chopped fresh parsley.
9. Roll up the pita bread or fold the flatbread to enclose the fillings.
10. Serve the Lebanese chicken shawarma as a delicious and flavorful wrap.

Nutritional Information per Serving (for the Chicken Shawarma):

- Calories: 280
- Proteins: 35g
- Fats: 10g
- Carbs: 10g
- Fiber: 2g
- Sugar: 2g
- Sodium: 400mg
- Omega 3: 0.3g

Italian Zucchini Boats with Ground Turkey

Servings: 4

Preparation Time: 15 minutes
Cooking Time: 25 minutes

Ingredients:

- Zucchini: 4 medium-sized
- Ground turkey: 1 pound (450g)
- Onion: 1 small, finely chopped
- Garlic: 2 cloves, minced
- Tomato sauce: 1 cup (240ml)
- Italian seasoning: 1 teaspoon
- Mozzarella cheese: ½ cup (60g), shredded
- Parmesan cheese: ¼ cup (25g), grated
- Fresh basil: 2 tablespoons, chopped
- Salt and pepper to taste

Instructions:

1. Preheat the oven to 400°F (200°C) and line a baking dish with foil.
2. Cut the zucchini in half lengthwise, and scoop out the flesh from the center of each half to create a hollow boat shape. Reserve the scooped-out zucchini flesh.
3. In a large skillet, cook the ground turkey over medium heat until browned and cooked through. Drain excess fat if needed.
4. Add the finely chopped onion and minced garlic to the skillet with the ground turkey. Sauté until the onion is translucent.
5. Chop the reserved zucchini flesh and add it to the skillet. Cook for another 2-3 minutes until softened.
6. Stir in the tomato sauce and Italian seasoning. Simmer for a few minutes to allow the flavors to meld. Season with salt and pepper to taste.
7. Fill each hollowed zucchini boat with the ground turkey mixture.
8. Place the filled zucchini boats in the prepared baking dish.
9. Sprinkle the shredded mozzarella cheese and grated Parmesan cheese over the top of each zucchini boat.

10. Bake in the preheated oven for 20-25 minutes, or until the zucchini is tender and the cheese is melted and golden.
11. Remove from the oven and let the zucchini boats cool for a few minutes.
12. Garnish with fresh chopped basil before serving.

Nutritional Information per Serving:

- Calories: 280
- Proteins: 30g
- Fats: 12g
- Carbs: 10g
- Fiber: 3g
- Sugar: 5g
- Sodium:420mg
- Omega 3: 0.3g

Greek Salad with Grilled Chicken

Servings: 4

Preparation Time: 15 minutes (+ marinating time)
Cooking Time: 15-20 minutes

Ingredients:

For the Grilled Chicken:
- Chicken breasts: 2, boneless and skinless
- Extra Virgin Olive Oil: 2 tablespoons
- Lemon juice: 2 tablespoons
- Garlic: 2 cloves, minced
- Dried oregano: 1 teaspoon
- Salt and pepper to taste

For the Greek Salad:
- Romaine lettuce: 1 head, chopped
- Cucumber: 1, diced
- Cherry tomatoes: 1 cup (150g), halved
- Red onion: 1 small, thinly sliced
- Kalamata olives: ½ cup (75g), pitted
- Feta cheese: ½ cup (60g), crumbled
- Fresh parsley: 2 tablespoons, chopped
- Extra Virgin Olive Oil: 2 tablespoons
- Red wine vinegar: 1 tablespoon
- Dried oregano: 1 teaspoon
- Salt and pepper to taste

Instructions:

1. In a bowl, whisk together the Extra Virgin Olive Oil, lemon juice, minced garlic, dried oregano, salt, and pepper to make the marinade for the grilled chicken.
2. Pound the chicken breasts to an even thickness and place them in a shallow dish. Pour the marinade over the chicken and let it marinate for at least 30 minutes, or up to overnight in the refrigerator.
3. Preheat the grill or grill pan over medium-high heat. Grill the marinated chicken breasts for 6-8 minutes per side, or until cooked through and grill marks appear. Let them rest for a few minutes before slicing.
4. In a large salad bowl, combine the chopped romaine lettuce, diced cucumber, halved cherry tomatoes, thinly sliced red onion, Kalamata olives, crumbled feta cheese, and chopped fresh parsley.
5. In a small bowl, whisk together the Extra Virgin Olive Oil, red wine vinegar, dried oregano, salt, and pepper to make the dressing.
6. Drizzle the dressing over the Greek salad and toss to coat the ingredients evenly.
7. Slice the grilled chicken breasts and arrange them on top of the Greek salad.
8. Serve the Greek salad with grilled chicken as a refreshing and satisfying meal.

Nutritional Information per Serving:

- Calories: 320
- Proteins: 30g
- Fats: 18g
- Carbs: 12g
- Fiber: 4g
- Sugar: 5g
- Sodium: 620mg
- Omega 3: 03g

By incorporating these low-carb recipes into your meal repertoire, you can enjoy delicious dinners without sacrificing your health and well-being. With the right ingredients and simple techniques, you can create flavorful and satisfying meals in no time. We encourage you to experiment with these recipes, make them your own, and discover new flavors and combinations along the way.

Remember, the beauty of effortless dinners lies in their simplicity. These recipes are designed to save you time and energy, so you can focus on enjoying the company of loved ones or indulging in some well-deserved relaxation.

Chapter 7. Snacks and Sides for Busy Days

In this chapter, we present a collection of delectable low-carb recipes that are perfect for those moments when you need a quick and satisfying snack or a flavorful side dish to accompany your meals. We understand that life can get hectic, and finding time to prepare nutritious and delicious snacks and sides can be a challenge. That's why we have curated a selection of recipes that are not only easy to make but also packed with flavor and wholesome ingredients.

Here, you'll find an array of options that will cater to your cravings and keep you fueled throughout the day. From savory bites to refreshing salads, these snacks and sides are designed to be enjoyed on the go or as a delightful addition to your main meals. We have carefully chosen ingredients that are nutrient-dense and low in carbs, making certain that you stay on track with your dietary goals while indulging in tasty treats.

Whether you're looking for a quick and satisfying snack to curb those mid-afternoon cravings or a side dish that complements your main course, this chapter has you covered. These recipes are designed to be fuss-free, allowing you to prepare them in a matter of minutes without compromising on taste or quality. So, get ready to learn a range of delightful snacks and sides that will enhance your low-carb lifestyle.

Cheesy Cauliflower Tots

Servings: 4

Preparation Time: 15 minutes
Cooking Time: 25 minutes

Ingredients:

- Cauliflower florets: 1 small head (about 4 cups)
- Cheddar cheese: 1 cup (120g), shredded
- Parmesan cheese: ½ cup (50g), grated
- Garlic powder: 1 teaspoon
- Onion powder: 1 teaspoon
- Dried parsley: 1 teaspoon
- Salt and pepper to taste
- Egg: 1, beaten

Instructions:

1. Preheat the oven to 400°F (200°C) and line a baking sheet with parchment paper.
2. Steam or boil the cauliflower florets until they are tender. Drain well and allow them to cool slightly.
3. Once the cauliflower has cooled, transfer it to a clean kitchen towel or cheesecloth. Squeeze out any excess moisture from the cauliflower, as this will help the tots hold together better.
4. Place the cauliflower in a mixing bowl and add the shredded cheddar cheese, grated Parmesan cheese, garlic powder, onion powder, dried parsley, salt, and pepper. Mix well to combine.
5. Add the beaten egg to the cauliflower mixture and stir until everything is evenly incorporated.
6. Take about a tablespoon of the mixture and shape it into a small cylindrical tot shape. Place it on the prepared baking sheet. Repeat this process with the remaining mixture, spacing the tots evenly apart.
7. Bake in the preheated oven for 20-25 minutes, or until the tots are golden brown and crispy on the outside.
8. Remove from the oven and let them cool for a few minutes before serving.
9. Serve the cheesy cauliflower tots as a delicious and low-carb snack or side dish.

Nutritional Information per Serving:

- Calories: 180
- Proteins: 10g
- Fats: 12g
- Carbs: 8g
- Fiber: 3g
- Sugar: 2g
- Sodium: 320mg
- Omega 3: 01.g

Mini Pepper Nachos

Servings: 4

Preparation Time: 15 minutes
Cooking Time: 15 minutes

Ingredients:

- Mini sweet peppers: 8
- Ground beef: ½ pound (225g)
- Onion: ½ small, finely diced
- Garlic: 2 cloves, minced
- Taco seasoning: 1 tablespoon
- Cherry tomatoes: ½ cup (75g), diced
- Jalapeño pepper: 1 small, seeded and finely diced
- Shredded cheddar cheese: ½ cup (60g)
- Guacamole: ½ cup (120g), for serving
- Sour cream: ½ cup (120g), for serving
- Fresh cilantro: for garnish
- Salt and pepper to taste

Instructions:

1. Preheat the oven to 400°F (200°C) and line a baking sheet with parchment paper.
2. Slice each mini sweet pepper in half lengthwise, and remove the seeds and membranes.
3. In a skillet, brown the ground beef over medium heat. Add the finely diced onion and minced garlic. Cook until the beef is fully cooked and the onion is translucent.
4. Drain any excess fat from the skillet. Add the taco seasoning, diced cherry tomatoes, and diced jalapeño pepper. Stir

well to combine and cook for an additional 2-3 minutes. Season with salt and pepper to taste.

5. Arrange the mini pepper halves on the prepared baking sheet, cut-side up.

6. Spoon the ground beef mixture into each mini pepper half, filling them evenly.

7. Sprinkle the shredded cheddar cheese over the top of each filled mini pepper.

8. Bake in the preheated oven for 10-12 minutes, or until the cheese is melted and bubbly.

9. Remove from the oven and let them cool slightly.

10. Serve the mini pepper nachos with a dollop of guacamole and sour cream. Garnish with fresh cilantro.

Nutritional Information per Serving:

- Calories: 250
- Proteins: 15g
- Fats: 17g
- Carbs: 9g
- Fiber: 2g
- Sugar: 5g
- Sodium: 450mg
- Omega 3: 0.2g

Zucchini Fritters with Sour Cream Dip

Servings: 4

Preparation Time: 15 minutes
Cooking Time: 15 minutes

Ingredients:

For the Zucchini Fritters:
- Zucchini: 2 medium-sized
- Salt: 1 teaspoon
- Egg: 1
- Garlic: 2 cloves, minced
- Fresh dill: 2 tablespoons, chopped
- Almond flour: ¼ cup (30g)
- Parmesan cheese: ¼ cup (25g), grated
- Black pepper to taste

- Extra Virgin Olive Oil: for frying

For the Sour Cream Dip:
- Sour cream: ½ cup (120g)
- Lemon juice: 1 tablespoon
- Dill: 1 tablespoon, chopped
- Salt and pepper to taste

Instructions:

1. Grate the zucchini using a box grater or food processor. Place the grated zucchini in a colander, sprinkle with salt, and let it sit for 10 minutes. Squeeze out any excess moisture from the zucchini using a clean kitchen towel or cheesecloth.

2. In a mixing bowl, combine the grated zucchini, egg, minced garlic, chopped fresh dill, almond flour, grated Parmesan cheese, and black pepper. Mix well until all the ingredients are evenly combined.

3. Heat a tablespoon of Extra Virgin Olive Oil in a large skillet over medium heat.

4. Take about two tablespoons of the zucchini mixture and shape it into a small fritter. Place it in the hot skillet and flatten it slightly with a spatula. Repeat this process to make several more fritters, leaving some space between each fritter in the skillet.

5. Cook the zucchini fritters for 3-4 minutes on each side, or until they are golden brown and crispy. You may need to cook them in batches depending on the size of your skillet. Add more Extra Virgin Olive Oil to the skillet as needed for subsequent batches.

6. Transfer the cooked fritters to a paper towel-lined plate to remove any excess oil.

7. In a small bowl, mix together the sour cream, lemon juice, chopped dill, salt, and pepper to make the sour cream dip.

8. Serve the zucchini fritters warm with the sour cream dip on the side.

Nutritional Information per Serving (4 Zucchini Fritters with Sour Cream Dip):

- Calories: 150
- Proteins: 6g
- Fats: 11g
- Carbs: 6g
- Fiber: 2g
- Sugar: 3g

- Sodium: 420mg
- Omega 3: 0.2g

- Calories: 150
- Proteins: 6g
- Fats: 12g
- Carbs: 2g
- Fiber: 1g
- Sugar: 1g
- Sodium: 400mg
- Omega 3: 0.1g

Bacon-Wrapped Asparagus Bundles

Servings: 4

Preparation Time: 10 minutes
Cooking Time: 20 minutes

Ingredients:

- Asparagus spears: 16 spears
- Bacon slices: 8 slices
- Extra Virgin Olive Oil: 2 tablespoons
- Garlic powder: 1 teaspoon
- Salt and pepper to taste

Instructions:

1. Preheat the oven to 400°F (200°C) and line a baking sheet with parchment paper.
2. Trim off the tough ends of the asparagus spears.
3. Divide the asparagus spears into 4 equal bundles, about 4 spears in each bundle.
4. Take a slice of bacon and wrap it tightly around each bundle, starting from one end and wrapping it in a spiral motion. Repeat this process for the remaining asparagus bundles.
5. Place the bacon-wrapped asparagus bundles on the prepared baking sheet.
6. Drizzle Extra Virgin Olive Oil over the bundles and sprinkle them with garlic powder, salt, and pepper.
7. Bake in the preheated oven for 18-20 minutes, or until the bacon is crispy and the asparagus is tender.
8. Remove from the oven and let them cool slightly before serving.
9. Serve the bacon-wrapped asparagus bundles as a delightful low-carb snack or as a side dish to accompany your main course.

Nutritional Information per Serving:

Buffalo Cauliflower Bites

Servings: 4

Preparation Time: 10 minutes
Cooking Time: 25 minutes

Ingredients:

- Cauliflower florets: 1 small head (about 4 cups)
- Extra Virgin Olive Oil: 2 tablespoons
- Garlic powder: 1 teaspoon
- Paprika: 1 teaspoon
- Salt and pepper to taste
- Hot sauce: ¼ cup (60ml)
- Butter: 2 tablespoons, melted
- Optional: Blue cheese or ranch dressing, for dipping

Instructions:

1. Preheat the oven to 450°F (230°C) and line a baking sheet with parchment paper.
2. Cut the cauliflower into bite-sized florets, discarding the tough stems.
3. In a large mixing bowl, combine the cauliflower florets, Extra Virgin Olive Oil, garlic powder, paprika, salt, and pepper. Toss well to evenly coat the cauliflower.
4. Spread the seasoned cauliflower florets onto the prepared baking sheet in a single layer.
5. Bake in the preheated oven for 20 minutes, or until the cauliflower is tender and slightly browned, flipping them halfway through.
6. In a separate bowl, whisk together the hot sauce and melted butter.

7. Remove the cauliflower from the oven and drizzle the hot sauce mixture over the roasted florets. Toss gently to coat the cauliflower evenly.

8. Return the baking sheet to the oven and bake for an additional 5 minutes to allow the sauce to adhere and create a slightly crispy coating.

9. Remove from the oven and let the buffalo cauliflower bites cool for a few minutes.

10. Serve the buffalo cauliflower bites as a delicious and low-carb snack. You can also serve them with blue cheese or ranch dressing for dipping, if desired.

Nutritional Information per Serving:

- Calories: 120
- Proteins: 3g
- Fats: 9g
- Carbs: 8g
- Fiber: 3g
- Sugar: 3g
- Sodium: 550mg
- Omega 3: 0.1g

Stuffed Bell Pepper Poppers

Servings: 4

Preparation Time: 15 minutes
Cooking Time: 15 minutes

Ingredients:

- Mini bell peppers: 8
- Cream cheese: 4 ounces (113g), softened
- Shredded cheddar cheese: ½ cup (60g)
- Green onions: 2, thinly sliced
- Garlic powder: 1 teaspoon
- Paprika: 1 teaspoon
- Salt and pepper to taste
- Optional: Ranch or sour cream, for dipping

Instructions:

1. Preheat the oven to 375°F (190°C) and line a baking sheet with parchment paper.

2. Cut the tops off the mini bell peppers and remove the seeds and membranes.

3. In a mixing bowl, combine the cream cheese, shredded cheddar cheese, sliced green onions, garlic powder, paprika, salt, and pepper. Mix well until all the ingredients are evenly incorporated.

4. Spoon the cream cheese mixture into each mini bell pepper, filling them to the top.

5. Place the stuffed bell pepper poppers on the prepared baking sheet.

6. Bake in the preheated oven for 12-15 minutes, or until the peppers are slightly softened and the cheese is melted and bubbly.

7. Remove from the oven and let them cool for a few minutes before serving.

8. Serve the stuffed bell pepper poppers as a flavorful and low-carb appetizer or snack. They can be enjoyed as is or paired with ranch or sour cream for dipping, if desired.

Nutritional Information per Serving:

- Calories: 120
- Proteins: 5g
- Fats: 8g
- Carbs: 6g
- Fiber: 1g
- Sugar: 3g
- Sodium: 180mg
- Omega 3: 0.1g

Loaded Avocado Fries

Servings: 4

Preparation Time: 20 minutes
Cooking Time: 15 minutes

Ingredients:

- Avocados: 2 large, ripe
- Almond flour: ½ cup (60g)
- Paprika: 1 teaspoon
- Garlic powder: 1 teaspoon
- Salt and pepper to taste
- Eggs: 2, beaten
- Bacon: 4 slices, cooked and crumbled
- Shredded cheddar cheese: ½ cup (60g)
- Sour cream: ¼ cup (60g), for serving
- Fresh cilantro: for garnish
- Optional: Lime wedges, for serving

Instructions:

1. Preheat the oven to 425°F (220°C) and line a baking sheet with parchment paper.
2. Cut the avocados in half, remove the pits, and slice each half into wedges.
3. In a shallow bowl, combine the almond flour, paprika, garlic powder, salt, and pepper. Mix well.
4. Dip each avocado wedge into the beaten eggs, then coat it with the almond flour mixture, pressing gently to adhere. Place the coated avocado wedges on the prepared baking sheet.
5. Bake in the preheated oven for 12-15 minutes, or until the avocado fries are golden brown and crispy.
6. Remove from the oven and let them cool slightly.
7. Sprinkle the cooked and crumbled bacon and shredded cheddar cheese over the avocado fries.
8. Return the baking sheet to the oven for an additional 3-4 minutes, or until the cheese is melted.
9. Remove from the oven and let the loaded avocado fries cool for a few minutes.
10. Serve the loaded avocado fries with a dollop of sour cream, fresh cilantro, and lime wedges on the side.

Nutritional Information per Serving:

- Calories: 250
- Proteins: 9g
- Fats: 21g
- Carbs: 8g
- Fiber: 7g
- Sugar: 1g
- Sodium: 320mg
- Omega 3: 0.1

Caprese Skewers with Balsamic Glaze

Servings: 4

Preparation Time: 15 minutes
Cooking Time: None

Ingredients:

- Cherry tomatoes: 16
- Fresh mozzarella cheese: 8 ounces (225g), cubed
- Fresh basil leaves: 16
- Balsamic glaze: 2 tablespoons
- Extra virgin Extra Virgin Olive Oil: 1 tablespoon
- Salt and pepper to taste
- Optional: Fresh basil leaves for garnish

Instructions:

1. Skewer one cherry tomato, one cube of mozzarella cheese, and one basil leaf onto each skewer, repeating until all the ingredients are used.
2. Arrange the caprese skewers on a serving platter.
3. In a small bowl, whisk together the balsamic glaze, extra virgin Extra Virgin Olive Oil, salt, and pepper.
4. Drizzle the balsamic glaze mixture over the caprese skewers.
5. Optional: Garnish with additional fresh basil leaves for added freshness and presentation.

6. Serve the caprese skewers with balsamic glaze as a delightful and refreshing low-carb snack or appetizer.

Nutritional Information per Serving (4 Caprese Skewers):

- Calories: 150
- Proteins: 9g
- Fats: 11g
- Carbs: 4g
- Fiber: 1g
- Sugar: 2g
- Sodium: 180mg
- Omega 3: 0.1g

Spinach and Artichoke Dip-Stuffed Mushrooms

Servings: 4

Preparation Time: 20 minutes
Cooking Time: 20 minutes

Ingredients:

- Cremini mushrooms: 16 large
- Extra Virgin Olive Oil: 2 tablespoons
- Garlic: 2 cloves, minced
- Spinach: 2 cups (60g), chopped
- Artichoke hearts: ½ cup (85g), chopped
- Cream cheese: 4 ounces (113g), softened
- Sour cream: ¼ cup (60g)
- Shredded mozzarella cheese: ¼ cup (25g)
- Grated Parmesan cheese: ¼ cup (25g)
- Salt and pepper to taste
- Optional: Fresh parsley for garnish

Instructions:

1. Preheat the oven to 375°F (190°C) and line a baking sheet with parchment paper.
2. Remove the stems from the cremini mushrooms and clean them with a damp cloth or paper towel. Set aside.
3. In a skillet, heat the Extra Virgin Olive Oil over medium heat. Add the minced garlic and sauté until fragrant, about 1 minute.
4. Add the chopped spinach to the skillet and cook until wilted, about 2-3 minutes.
5. Remove the skillet from heat and let the spinach cool slightly. Once cooled, squeeze out any excess moisture from the spinach.
6. In a mixing bowl, combine the cooked spinach, chopped artichoke hearts, softened cream cheese, sour cream, shredded mozzarella cheese, grated Parmesan cheese, salt, and pepper. Mix well until all the ingredients are thoroughly combined.
7. Stuff each cremini mushroom cap with a generous amount of the spinach and artichoke dip mixture, filling them to the top.
8. Place the stuffed mushrooms on the prepared baking sheet.

9. Bake in the preheated oven for 18-20 minutes, or until the mushrooms are tender and the filling is golden and bubbly.
10. Remove from the oven and let them cool for a few minutes before serving.
11. Optional: Garnish with fresh parsley for added freshness and presentation.
12. Serve the spinach and artichoke dip-stuffed mushrooms as a delicious and satisfying low-carb appetizer or side dish.

Nutritional Information per Serving
(4 Stuffed Mushrooms):

- Calories: 120
- Proteins: 6g
- Fats: 9g
- Carbs: 6g
- Fiber: 2g
- Sugar: 1g
- Sodium: 220mg
- Omega 3: 0.1g

Cucumber and Smoked Salmon Roll-Ups

Servings: 4

Preparation Time: 15 minutes

Ingredients:

- English cucumber: 1
- Smoked salmon: 4 ounces (113g)
- Cream cheese: 4 ounces (113g), softened
- Fresh dill: 2 tablespoons, chopped
- Lemon juice: 1 tablespoon
- Salt and pepper to taste

Instructions:

1. Wash the English cucumber and cut it into thin lengthwise strips using a mandoline slicer or a vegetable peeler.
2. Lay out the cucumber strips on a clean surface or cutting board.

3. Spread a thin layer of softened cream cheese onto each cucumber strip.
4. Place a slice of smoked salmon onto each cucumber strip, slightly overlapping it with the cream cheese layer.
5. Sprinkle fresh dill over the smoked salmon layer.
6. Drizzle lemon juice over the cucumber and smoked salmon roll-ups.
7. Season with salt and pepper to taste.
8. Starting from one end, tightly roll up each cucumber strip with the cream cheese, smoked salmon, and dill inside.
9. Repeat this process for the remaining cucumber strips.
10. Arrange the cucumber and smoked salmon roll-ups on a serving platter.
11. Optional: Garnish with additional fresh dill for added freshness and presentation.
12. Serve the cucumber and smoked salmon roll-ups as a light and refreshing low-carb snack or appetizer.

Nutritional Information per Serving:

- Calories: 150
- Proteins: 9g
- Fats: 11g
- Carbs: 3g
- Fiber: 1g
- Sugar: 2g
- Sodium: 350mg
- Omega 3: 0.2g

Greek Salad Skewers

Servings: 4

Preparation Time: 15 minutes

Ingredients:

- Cherry tomatoes: 16
- Cucumber: 1, cut into bite-sized cubes
- Kalamata olives: ½ cup (85g), pitted
- Feta cheese: 4 ounces (113g), cubed
- Red onion: ½ small, thinly sliced
- Greek salad dressing: ¼ cup (60ml)
- Fresh parsley: for garnish

- Wooden skewers: 8

Instructions:

1. Prepare the wooden skewers by soaking them in water for about 15 minutes to prevent them from burning.
2. Thread the ingredients onto the skewers in a desired pattern. Start with a cherry tomato, followed by a cube of cucumber, a kalamata olive, a cube of feta cheese, and a slice of red onion. Repeat this pattern until the skewer is filled.
3. Arrange the Greek salad skewers on a serving platter.
4. Drizzle Greek salad dressing over the skewers, ensuring all the ingredients are coated.
5. Optional: Garnish with fresh parsley for added freshness and presentation.
6. Serve the Greek salad skewers as a flavorful and refreshing low-carb snack or appetizer.

Nutritional Information per Serving (4 Skewers):

- Calories: 120
- Proteins: 5g
- Fats: 8g
- Carbs: 6g
- Fiber: 2g
- Sugar: 2g
- Sodium: 350mg
- Omega 3: 0.1g

Herbed Feta Stuffed Cherry Tomatoes

Servings: 4

Preparation Time: 15 minutes

Ingredients:

- Cherry tomatoes: 16
- Feta cheese: 4 ounces (113g), crumbled
- Fresh basil: ¼ cup (15g), finely chopped
- Fresh parsley: ¼ cup (15g), finely chopped
- Garlic powder: ½ teaspoon
- Extra Virgin Olive Oil: 2 tablespoons
- Salt and pepper to taste

Instructions:

1. Cut off the top of each cherry tomato and scoop out the seeds and pulp using a small spoon or a knife. Set aside.
2. In a mixing bowl, combine the crumbled feta cheese, finely chopped fresh basil, finely chopped fresh parsley, garlic powder, Extra Virgin Olive Oil, salt, and pepper. Mix well until all the ingredients are thoroughly combined.
3. Spoon the herbed feta mixture into each hollowed cherry tomato, filling them to the top.
4. Arrange the stuffed cherry tomatoes on a serving platter.
5. Optional: Drizzle a small amount of Extra Virgin Olive Oil over the tomatoes for added flavor and presentation.
6. Serve the herbed feta stuffed cherry tomatoes as a delightful and flavorful low-carb snack or appetizer.

Nutritional Information per Serving (4 Stuffed Cherry Tomatoes):

- Calories: 80
- Proteins: 5g
- Fats: 6g
- Carbs: 2g
- Fiber: 1g
- Sugar: 1g
- Sodium: 200mg
- Omega 3: 0.1g

Baba Ganoush with Fresh Veggies

Servings: 4

Preparation Time: 15 minutes
Cooking Time: 40 minutes

Ingredients:

- Eggplant: 1 large
- Lemon juice: 2 tablespoons
- Tahini: 2 tablespoons
- Garlic: 2 cloves, minced
- Extra virgin Extra Virgin Olive Oil: 2 tablespoons, plus more for drizzling
- Salt and pepper to taste
- Fresh parsley: for garnish
- Assorted fresh veggies (e.g., cucumber, bell peppers, carrot sticks): for dipping

Instructions:

1. Preheat the oven to 400°F (200°C).
2. Pierce the eggplant several times with a fork and place it on a baking sheet lined with parchment paper.
3. Roast the eggplant in the preheated oven for 35-40 minutes, or until the skin is charred and the flesh is soft.
4. Remove the eggplant from the oven and let it cool for a few minutes.
5. Once the eggplant is cool enough to handle, cut it in half lengthwise and scoop out the flesh with a spoon, discarding the charred skin.
6. Place the eggplant flesh in a colander or sieve and allow any excess liquid to drain for about 10 minutes.
7. In a food processor or blender, combine the drained eggplant flesh, lemon juice, tahini, minced garlic, extra virgin Extra Virgin Olive Oil, salt, and pepper. Blend until smooth and creamy.
8. Taste and adjust the seasonings, if needed.
9. Transfer the baba ganoush to a serving bowl and drizzle with a little extra virgin Extra Virgin Olive Oil.
10. Optional: Garnish with fresh parsley for added freshness and presentation.

11. Serve the baba ganoush with fresh veggies as a delicious and healthy low-carb dip.

Nutritional Information per Serving (without veggies):

- Calories: 80
- Proteins: 2g
- Fats: 7g
- Carbs: 4g
- Fiber: 2g
- Sugar: 1g
- Sodium: 60mg
- Omega 3: 0.2g

Mediterranean Hummus Platter

Servings: 4

Preparation Time: 10 minutes

Ingredients:

- Hummus: 1 cup (240g)
- Cherry tomatoes: 1 cup (150g), halved
- Cucumber: 1, sliced
- Kalamata olives: ½ cup (85g), pitted
- Feta cheese: ½ cup (60g), crumbled
- Red onion: ½ small, thinly sliced
- Extra virgin Extra Virgin Olive Oil: 2 tablespoons
- Lemon juice: 1 tablespoon
- Fresh parsley: for garnish
- Pita bread or pita chips: for serving

Instructions:

1. Start by spreading the hummus on a large serving platter or a shallow bowl.
2. Arrange the cherry tomatoes, cucumber slices, kalamata olives, crumbled feta cheese, and thinly sliced red onion on top of the hummus.

3. Drizzle the extra virgin Extra Virgin Olive Oil and lemon juice over the ingredients on the platter.
4. Optional: Garnish with fresh parsley for added freshness and presentation.
5. Serve the Mediterranean hummus platter with pita bread or pita chips for dipping.
6. Enjoy the variety of flavors and textures in this delightful low-carb snack or appetizer.

Nutritional Information per Serving
(without pita bread/chips):

- Calories: 200
- Proteins: 6g
- Fats: 16g
- Carbs: 10g
- Fiber: 4g
- Sugar: 2g
- Sodium: 500mg
- Omega 3: 0.3g

Tzatziki Cucumber Bites

Servings: 4

Preparation Time: 15 minutes

Ingredients:

- English cucumber: 1
- Greek yogurt: ½ cup (120g)
- Cucumber: ½ small, finely diced
- Garlic: 1 clove, minced
- Fresh dill: 1 tablespoon, chopped
- Lemon juice: 1 tablespoon
- Salt and pepper to taste
- Optional: Fresh dill or paprika for garnish

Instructions:

1. Wash the English cucumber and cut it into thick slices, about 1 inch thick.
2. Use a small spoon or a melon baller to scoop out a small hollow in the center of each cucumber slice, creating a cup-like shape.
3. In a mixing bowl, combine the Greek yogurt, finely diced cucumber, minced garlic, chopped fresh dill, lemon juice, salt, and pepper. Stir well to combine all the ingredients.
4. Spoon a small amount of the tzatziki mixture into each cucumber cup, filling it to the top.
5. Optional: Garnish with fresh dill or a sprinkle of paprika for added freshness and presentation.
6. Serve the tzatziki cucumber bites as a refreshing and flavorful low-carb snack or appetizer.

Nutritional Information per Serving
(4 Cucumber Bites):

- Calories: 60
- Proteins: 4g
- Fats: 1g
- Carbs: 7g
- Fiber: 1g
- Sugar: 4g
- Sodium: 60mg
- Omega 3: 0.1g

Olive and Cheese Stuffed Mini Peppers

Servings: 4

Preparation Time: 15 minutes

Ingredients:

- Mini bell peppers: 12
- Cream cheese: 4 ounces (113g), softened
- Black olives: ¼ cup (30g), sliced
- Feta cheese: ¼ cup (30g), crumbled
- Fresh parsley: 2 tablespoons, chopped
- Extra Virgin Olive Oil: 1 tablespoon
- Lemon juice: 1 tablespoon
- Salt and pepper to taste

Instructions:

1. Wash the mini bell peppers and slice off the tops. Remove the seeds and membranes from inside each pepper.
2. In a mixing bowl, combine the softened cream cheese, sliced black olives, crumbled feta cheese, chopped fresh parsley, Extra Virgin Olive Oil, lemon juice, salt, and pepper. Mix well until all the ingredients are thoroughly combined.
3. Spoon the cheese and olive mixture into each mini bell pepper, filling them to the top.
4. Arrange the stuffed mini peppers on a serving platter.
5. Optional: Drizzle a small amount of Extra Virgin Olive Oil over the peppers for added flavor and presentation.
6. Serve the olive and cheese stuffed mini peppers as a savory and delicious low-carb snack or appetizer.

Nutritional Information per Serving
(3 Stuffed Mini Peppers):

- Calories: 100
- Proteins: 5g
- Fats: 8g
- Carbs: 4g
- Fiber: 1g
- Sugar: 2g
- Sodium: 200mg
- Omega 3: 0.1g

Greek Yogurt Parfait with Berries and Nuts

Servings: 2

Preparation Time: 10 minutes

Ingredients:

- Greek yogurt: 1 cup (240g)
- Mixed berries (e.g., strawberries, blueberries, raspberries): 1 cup (150g)
- Mixed nuts (e.g., almonds, walnuts, pistachios): ¼ cup (30g), chopped
- Honey: 2 tablespoons
- Optional: Fresh mint leaves for garnish

Instructions:

1. In two serving glasses or bowls, start by layering half of the Greek yogurt in each.
2. Top the yogurt with a layer of mixed berries, using half of the berries in each glass.
3. Sprinkle a portion of the chopped mixed nuts over the berries in each glass.
4. Drizzle a tablespoon of honey over each parfait.
5. Repeat the layering process, starting with the remaining Greek yogurt, followed by the remaining mixed berries, and then the remaining chopped mixed nuts.
6. Drizzle another tablespoon of honey over each parfait.
7. Optional: Garnish with fresh mint leaves for added freshness and presentation.
8. Serve the Greek yogurt parfait with berries and nuts as a delightful and nutritious low-carb snack or dessert.

Nutritional Information per Serving:

- Calories: 250
- Proteins: 15g
- Fats: 13
- Carbs: 20g
- Fiber: 4g
- Sugar: 13g
- Sodium: 80mg
- Omega 3: 0.4g

Roasted Eggplant and Red Pepper Dip

Servings: 4

Preparation Time: 10 minutes
Cooking Time: 40 minutes

Ingredients:

- Eggplant: 1 large
- Red bell pepper: 1
- Garlic: 2 cloves
- Tahini: 2 tablespoons
- Lemon juice: 2 tablespoons
- Extra Virgin Olive Oil: 2 tablespoons
- Salt and pepper to taste
- Optional: Fresh parsley for garnish
- Optional: Pita bread or vegetable sticks for serving

Instructions:

1. Preheat the oven to 400°F (200°C).
2. Pierce the eggplant and red bell pepper several times with a fork and place them on a baking sheet lined with parchment paper.
3. Roast the eggplant and red bell pepper in the preheated oven for about 40 minutes, or until the skin is charred and the flesh is soft.
4. Remove the baking sheet from the oven and let the eggplant and red bell pepper cool for a few minutes.
5. Once cooled, cut off the stem of the eggplant and peel off the skin. Remove the seeds and stem from the red bell pepper.
6. In a food processor or blender, combine the roasted eggplant, roasted red bell pepper, garlic cloves, tahini, lemon juice, Extra Virgin Olive Oil, salt, and pepper. Blend until smooth and creamy.
7. Taste and adjust the seasonings, if needed.
8. Transfer the roasted eggplant and red pepper dip to a serving bowl.
9. Optional: Garnish with fresh parsley for added freshness and presentation.
10. Serve the dip with pita bread or vegetable sticks for dipping.

Nutritional Information per Serving
(without pita bread/vegetable sticks):

- Calories: 90
- Proteins: 2g
- Fats: 7g
- Carbs: 7g
- Fiber: 2g
- Sugar: 4g
- Sodium: 150mg
- Omega 3: 0.1g

Stuffed Grape Leaves (Dolmades)

Servings: 4

Preparation Time: 30 minutes
Cooking Time: 40 minutes

Ingredients:

- Grape leaves: 24
- Rice: ½ cup (90g), rinsed
- Onion: ½ small, finely chopped
- Fresh dill: 2 tablespoons, chopped
- Fresh parsley: 2 tablespoons, chopped
- Lemon juice: 2 tablespoons
- Extra virgin Extra Virgin Olive Oil: 2 tablespoons
- Salt and pepper to taste
- Water: 1 cup (240ml)

Instructions:

1. Rinse the grape leaves under cold water to remove any brine or excess salt. If using canned grape leaves, gently separate them and rinse.
2. In a mixing bowl, combine the rinsed rice, finely chopped onion, chopped fresh dill, chopped fresh parsley, lemon juice, extra virgin Extra Virgin Olive Oil, salt, and pepper. Mix well until all the ingredients are thoroughly combined.
3. Place a grape leaf on a clean surface, shiny side down. Add a small spoonful of the rice mixture near the stem end of the leaf.

4. Fold the sides of the leaf over the filling and roll it tightly into a small cylinder shape.
5. Repeat the process with the remaining grape leaves and rice mixture.
6. Place the stuffed grape leaves in a large pot, seam side down, in a single layer.
7. Pour water over the stuffed grape leaves, making sure they are fully covered.
8. Place a heatproof plate or a lid on top of the stuffed grape leaves to keep them submerged during cooking.
9. Cover the pot and bring the water to a boil over medium heat. Reduce the heat to low and simmer for 40 minutes, or until the rice is cooked and the grape leaves are tender.
10. Remove the stuffed grape leaves from the pot and let them cool slightly before serving.
11. Optional: Drizzle with a little extra virgin Extra Virgin Olive Oil and garnish with fresh parsley for added flavor and presentation.
12. Serve the stuffed grape leaves as a delicious and traditional low-carb snack or appetizer.

Nutritional Information per Serving (6 Stuffed Grape Leaves):

- Calories: 150
- Proteins: 2g
- Fats: 6g
- Carbs: 22g
- Fiber: 2g
- Sugar: 2g
- Sodium: 200mg
- Omega 3: 0.1g

Aegean Style Cauliflower Rice Tabbouleh

Servings: 4

Preparation Time: 15 minutes

Ingredients:

- Cauliflower: 1 small head
- Cherry tomatoes: 1 cup (150g), halved
- Cucumber: 1, diced
- Red onion: ¼ cup (40g), finely chopped
- Fresh parsley: ½ cup (15g), chopped
- Fresh mint: ¼ cup (10g), chopped
- Lemon juice: 2 tablespoons
- Extra virgin Extra Virgin Olive Oil: 2 tablespoons
- Salt and pepper to taste

Instructions:

1. Remove the leaves and tough stem from the cauliflower head. Cut the cauliflower into florets.
2. Place the cauliflower florets in a food processor and pulse until they resemble rice-like grains. Be careful not to overprocess and turn it into a puree.
3. Transfer the cauliflower rice to a mixing bowl.
4. Add the cherry tomatoes, diced cucumber, finely chopped red onion, chopped fresh parsley, chopped fresh mint, lemon juice, extra virgin Extra Virgin Olive Oil, salt, and pepper to the cauliflower rice. Mix well to combine all the ingredients.
5. Taste and adjust the seasonings, if needed.
6. Serve the Greek Style Cauliflower Rice Tabbouleh as a refreshing and low-carb side dish or salad.

Nutritional Information per Serving:

- Calories: 60
- Proteins: 3g
- Fats: 4g
- Carbs: 7g
- Fiber: 3g
- Sugar: 3g
- Sodium: 50mg
- Omega 3: 0.1g

Chapter 8. Tasty Desserts with a Healthy Twist.

Who said you can't indulge in delicious desserts while following a low-carb diet? Here's a collection of mouthwatering recipes that are both tasty and nutritious. These desserts are designed to satisfy your sweet tooth without compromising your health and fitness goals. Get ready to embark on a delightful journey of guilt-free treats that will leave you feeling satisfied and energized. Whether you're a chocolate lover, a fruit enthusiast, or a fan of creamy delights, there's something here for everyone. So, let's dive in and discover these scrumptious desserts that are as good for your taste buds as they are for your body!

Chocolate Avocado Mousse

Servings: 4

Preparation Time: 10 minutes
Chilling Time: 2 hours

Ingredients:

- Ripe avocados: 2
- Unsweetened cocoa powder: ¼ cup (25g)
- Unsweetened almond milk: ½ cup (120ml)
- Maple syrup or sweetener of choice: ¼ cup (60ml)
- Vanilla extract: 1 teaspoon
- Optional toppings: Fresh berries, chopped nuts, or shredded coconut

Instructions:

1. Cut the avocados in half, remove the pits, and scoop out the flesh into a blender or food processor.
2. Add the unsweetened cocoa powder, almond milk, maple syrup (or sweetener of choice), and vanilla extract to the blender or food processor.
3. Blend until smooth and creamy, scraping down the sides as needed to ensure all the ingredients are well combined.
4. Taste and adjust the sweetness if desired.
5. Transfer the chocolate avocado mousse to serving glasses or bowls.
6. Cover and refrigerate for at least 2 hours to allow the mousse to set.
7. Prior to serving, you can top the mousse with fresh berries, chopped nuts, or shredded coconut for added flavor and texture.
8. Serve chilled and enjoy this indulgent and nutritious chocolate avocado mousse!

Nutritional Information per Serving:

- Calories: 170
- Proteins: 3g
- Fats: 13g
- Carbs: 14g
- Fiber: 7g
- Sugar: 4g
- Sodium: 5mg
- Omega 3: 0.3g

Peanut Butter Chocolate Chip Cookies

Servings: 12 cookies

Preparation Time: 10 minutes
Baking Time: 12-15 minutes

Ingredients:

- Natural peanut butter: ½ cup (120g)
- Erythritol or sweetener of choice: ⅓ cup (60g)
- Egg: 1
- Almond flour: 1 cup (100g)
- Baking powder: ½ teaspoon
- Salt: ¼ teaspoon
- Dark chocolate chips: ⅓ cup (60g)
- Optional: Chopped peanuts for extra crunch

Instructions:

1. Preheat the oven to 350°F (175°C) and line a baking sheet with parchment paper.
2. In a mixing bowl, combine the natural peanut butter and erythritol (or sweetener of choice). Mix well until smooth and creamy.
3. Add the egg to the peanut butter mixture and mix until fully incorporated.
4. In a separate bowl, whisk together the almond flour, baking powder, and salt.
5. Gradually add the dry ingredients to the peanut butter mixture, mixing until a thick dough forms.
6. Fold in the dark chocolate chips and chopped peanuts, if desired.
7. Scoop out about 1.5 tablespoons of dough per cookie and place them onto the prepared baking sheet. Flatten each cookie slightly with a fork.
8. Bake in the preheated oven for 12-15 minutes, or until the edges are golden brown.
9. Remove from the oven and let the cookies cool on the baking sheet for a few minutes, then transfer them to a wire rack to cool completely.
10. Once cooled, enjoy these delightful low-carb Peanut Butter Chocolate Chip Cookies

with a tall glass of almond milk or your favorite beverage.

Nutritional Information per Serving (1 Cookie):

- Calories: 140
- Proteins: 5g
- Fats: 11g
- Carbs: 6g
- Fiber: 2g
- Sugar: 1g
- Sodium: 90mg
- Omega 3: 0.1g

Lemon Blueberry Cheesecake Bars

Servings: 9 bars

Preparation Time: 15 minutes
Baking Time: 25-30 minutes
Chilling Time: 2 hours

Ingredients:

For the crust:
- Almond flour: 1 cup (100g)
- Coconut flour: 2 tablespoons
- Erythritol or sweetener of choice: 2 tablespoons
- Melted butter: 4 tablespoons

For the filling:
- Cream cheese: 8 ounces (225g), softened
- Erythritol or sweetener of choice: ¼ cup (40g)
- Lemon juice: 2 tablespoons
- Lemon zest: 1 teaspoon
- Vanilla extract: 1 teaspoon
- Eggs: 2

For the blueberry swirl:
- Fresh blueberries: ½ cup (75g)
- Erythritol or sweetener of choice: 1 tablespoon
- Lemon juice: 1 tablespoon

Instructions:

1. Preheat the oven to 325°F (160°C) and line an 8x8-inch baking pan with parchment paper.
2. In a mixing bowl, combine the almond flour, coconut flour, erythritol (or sweetener of choice), and melted butter for the crust. Mix until well combined.
3. Press the crust mixture evenly into the bottom of the prepared baking pan.
4. In a separate bowl, beat the cream cheese, erythritol (or sweetener of choice), lemon juice, lemon zest, and vanilla extract until smooth and creamy.
5. Add the eggs, one at a time, beating well after each addition.
6. Pour the cream cheese filling over the crust in the baking pan, spreading it evenly.
7. In a small saucepan, combine the fresh blueberries, erythritol (or sweetener of choice), and lemon juice for the blueberry swirl. Cook over low heat, stirring occasionally, until the blueberries soften and release their juices. Remove from heat and let it cool slightly.
8. Using a spoon, drop dollops of the blueberry mixture onto the cream cheese filling. Use a toothpick or a knife to swirl the blueberry mixture into the filling, creating a marbled effect.
9. Bake in the preheated oven for 25-30 minutes, or until the edges are set and the center is slightly jiggly.
10. Remove from the oven and let it cool completely in the pan.
11. Once cooled, refrigerate for at least 2 hours to allow the bars to set.
12. Cut into squares and serve these luscious Lemon Blueberry Cheesecake Bars as a refreshing and guilt-free dessert.

Nutritional Information per Serving (1 Bar):

- Calories: 220
- Proteins: 7g
- Fats: 19g
- Carbs: 6g
- Fiber: 2g
- Sugar: 3g
- Sodium: 170mg
- Omega 3: 0.1g

Almond Flour Brownies

Servings: 12 brownies

Preparation Time: 10 minutes
Baking Time: 20-25 minutes

Ingredients:

- Almond flour: 1 cup (100g)
- Unsweetened cocoa powder: ⅓ cup (30g)
- Erythritol or sweetener of choice: ½ cup (80g)
- Baking powder: 1 teaspoon
- Salt: ¼ teaspoon
- Unsweetened applesauce: ½ cup (120g)
- Melted butter or coconut oil: ¼ cup (60ml)
- Eggs: 2
- Vanilla extract: 1 teaspoon
- Optional: Chopped nuts or sugar-free chocolate chips for topping

Instructions:

1. Preheat the oven to 350°F (175°C) and line an 8x8-inch baking pan with parchment paper.
2. In a mixing bowl, whisk together the almond flour, unsweetened cocoa powder, erythritol (or sweetener of choice), baking powder, and salt.
3. In a separate bowl, combine the unsweetened applesauce, melted butter (or coconut oil), eggs, and vanilla extract. Mix well.
4. Add the wet ingredients to the dry ingredients and stir until all the ingredients are well combined.
5. Pour the batter into the prepared baking pan, spreading it evenly.
6. Optional: Sprinkle chopped nuts or sugar-free chocolate chips on top of the batter.
7. Bake in the preheated oven for 20-25 minutes, or until a toothpick inserted into the center comes out with a few moist crumbs.
8. Remove from the oven and let the brownies cool completely in the pan.
9. Once cooled, cut into squares and enjoy these rich and fudgy Almond Flour Brownies as a delightful low-carb dessert or snack.

Nutritional Information per Serving (1 Brownie):

- Calories: 110
- Proteins: 4g
- Fats: 9g
- Carbs: 6g
- Fiber: 2g
- Sugar: 1g
- Sodium: 85mg
- Omega 3: 0.1g

Strawberry Shortcake Parfait

Servings: 4 parfaits

Preparation Time: 15 minutes
Assembly Time: 10 minutes
Chilling Time: 1 hour

Ingredients:

- Almond flour: 1 cup (100g)
- Erythritol or sweetener of choice: 2 tablespoons
- Melted butter: 4 tablespoons
- Fresh strawberries: 2 cups (300g), sliced
- Heavy cream: 1 cup (240ml)
- Vanilla extract: 1 teaspoon
- Optional: Additional sweetener for the whipped cream, if desired

Instructions:

1. In a mixing bowl, combine the almond flour, erythritol (or sweetener of choice), and melted butter for the shortcake crumble. Mix until well combined.
2. Divide the mixture evenly among four serving glasses or bowls, creating a layer of the shortcake crumble at the bottom.
3. In a separate bowl, whip the heavy cream and vanilla extract until soft peaks form. Optional: Sweeten the whipped cream with additional sweetener if desired.
4. Spoon a dollop of whipped cream onto the shortcake crumble in each serving glass.
5. Add a layer of sliced strawberries on top of the whipped cream.
6. Repeat the layers until all the ingredients are used, finishing with a layer of whipped cream and a few strawberry slices on top.
7. Optional: Garnish with a sprinkle of almond flour or a fresh mint leaf.
8. Cover the parfaits and refrigerate for at least 1 hour to allow the flavors to meld and the shortcake crumble to soften slightly.
9. Serve these delightful Strawberry Shortcake Parfaits chilled and enjoy the perfect balance of creamy, fruity, and crumbly goodness.

Nutritional Information per Serving:

- Calories: 290
- Proteins: 5g
- Fats: 27g
- Carbs: 9g
- Fiber: 3g
- Sugar: 4g
- Sodium: 25mg
- Omega 3: 0.1g

Pumpkin Spice Chia Pudding

Servings: 2 servings

Preparation Time: 10 minutes
Chilling Time: 4 hours or overnight

Ingredients:

- Chia seeds: ¼ cup (40g)
- Unsweetened almond milk: 1 cup (240ml)
- Pumpkin puree: ½ cup (120g)
- Erythritol or sweetener of choice: 2 tablespoons
- Pumpkin pie spice: 1 teaspoon
- Vanilla extract: 1 teaspoon
- Optional toppings: Chopped nuts, coconut flakes, or a sprinkle of cinnamon

Instructions:

1. In a bowl, combine the chia seeds, unsweetened almond milk, pumpkin puree, erythritol (or sweetener of choice), pumpkin pie spice, and vanilla extract. Mix well until all the ingredients are thoroughly combined.
2. Let the mixture sit for 5 minutes, then give it another stir to prevent clumping of the chia seeds.
3. Cover the bowl and refrigerate for at least 4 hours or overnight, allowing the chia seeds to absorb the liquid and form a pudding-like consistency.

4. After chilling, give the chia pudding a good stir to evenly distribute any settled ingredients.
5. Divide the pumpkin spice chia pudding into serving bowls or glasses.
6. Optional: Top the pudding with chopped nuts, coconut flakes, or a sprinkle of cinnamon for added texture and flavor.
7. Serve chilled and enjoy this creamy and flavorful Pumpkin Spice Chia Pudding as a nutritious and satisfying dessert or snack.

Nutritional Information per Serving:

- Calories: 150
- Proteins: 6g
- Fats: 8g
- Carbs: 13g
- Fiber: 9g
- Sugar: 2g
- Sodium: 75mg
- Omega 3: 2g

Raspberry Almond Thumbprint Cookies

Servings: 12 cookies

Preparation Time: 10 minutes

Baking Time: 12-15 minutes

Ingredients:

- Almond flour: 1 cup (100g)
- Erythritol or sweetener of choice: ¼ cup (40g)
- Butter, softened: 4 tablespoons
- Almond extract: ½ teaspoon
- Raspberry jam or sugar-free fruit spread: ¼ cup (60g)

Instructions:

1. Preheat the oven to 350°F (175°C) and line a baking sheet with parchment paper.
2. In a mixing bowl, combine the almond flour, erythritol (or sweetener of choice), softened butter, and almond extract. Mix until the ingredients are well combined and a dough forms.
3. Roll the dough into 12 equal-sized balls and place them on the prepared baking sheet.
4. Use your thumb or the back of a spoon to create an indentation in the center of each cookie.
5. Spoon about ½ teaspoon of raspberry jam or sugar-free fruit spread into each indentation.
6. Bake in the preheated oven for 12-15 minutes, or until the edges of the cookies are golden brown.
7. Remove from the oven and let the cookies cool on the baking sheet for a few minutes, then transfer them to a wire rack to cool completely.
8. Once cooled, these delightful Raspberry Almond Thumbprint Cookies are ready to be enjoyed as a sweet and guilt-free treat.

Nutritional Information per Serving (1 Cookie):

- Calories: 90g
- Proteins: 2g
- Fats: 8g
- Carbs: 2g
- Fiber: 1g
- Sugar: 1g
- Sodium: 35mg
- Omega 3: 0.1g

Coconut Flour Pancakes with Berries

Servings: 2 servings (4 small pancakes)

Preparation Time: 10 minutes
Cooking Time: 10 minutes

Ingredients:

- Coconut flour: ¼ cup (30g)
- Baking powder: ½ teaspoon
- Erythritol or sweetener of choice: 2 tablespoons
- Salt: ⅛ teaspoon
- Eggs: 2
- Unsweetened almond milk: ¼ cup (60ml)
- Vanilla extract: ½ teaspoon
- Coconut oil or butter for cooking
- Fresh berries of choice for topping

Instructions:

1. In a mixing bowl, whisk together the coconut flour, baking powder, erythritol (or sweetener of choice), and salt.
2. In a separate bowl, whisk the eggs, unsweetened almond milk, and vanilla extract until well combined.
3. Add the wet ingredients to the dry ingredients and stir until a smooth batter forms. Let the batter sit for a few minutes to allow the coconut flour to absorb the liquid.
4. Heat a non-stick skillet or griddle over medium heat and grease it with coconut oil or butter.
5. Spoon about 2 tablespoons of batter onto the skillet to form a small pancake. Repeat to make additional pancakes, leaving space between them.
6. Cook the pancakes for about 2-3 minutes on one side, or until bubbles form on the surface. Flip the pancakes and cook for an additional 2-3 minutes on the other side, or until golden brown.
7. Transfer the cooked pancakes to a plate and repeat the process with the remaining batter.
8. Serve the Coconut Flour Pancakes with fresh berries of your choice on top. Drizzle with sugar-free syrup or a dollop of Greek yogurt, if desired.
9. Enjoy these fluffy and flavorful Coconut Flour Pancakes with Berries as a delightful low-carb breakfast or brunch option.

Nutritional Information per Serving
(2 Pancakes):

- Calories: 120
- Proteins: 6g
- Fats: 6g
- Carbs: 10g
- Fiber: 6g
- Sugar: 2g
- Sodium: 200mg:
- Omega 3: 0.2g

Vanilla Bean Panna Cotta

Servings: 4 servings

Preparation Time: 15 minutes
Chilling Time: 4 hours or overnight

Ingredients:

- Heavy cream: 1 cup (240ml)
- Unsweetened almond milk: 1 cup (240ml)
- Erythritol or sweetener of choice: ¼ cup (40g)
- Gelatin powder: 1 ½ teaspoons
- Vanilla bean pod, split lengthwise and seeds scraped (or 1 teaspoon pure vanilla extract)
- Fresh berries or sugar-free fruit sauce for topping

Instructions:

1. In a small saucepan, combine the heavy cream, almond milk, and erythritol (or sweetener of choice). Heat the mixture over low heat until it starts to simmer, stirring occasionally.
2. Meanwhile, sprinkle the gelatin powder over 2 tablespoons of cold water in a small bowl. Let it sit for a few minutes to bloom.
3. Remove the saucepan from heat and add the gelatin mixture, stirring until the gelatin is completely dissolved.
4. Add the scraped vanilla bean seeds or vanilla extract to the mixture and stir well to incorporate.
5. Divide the panna cotta mixture among four ramekins or dessert glasses.
6. Let the panna cotta cool to room temperature, then cover and refrigerate for at least 4 hours or overnight to set.
7. To serve, gently run a knife around the edges of the ramekins or glasses to loosen the panna cotta. Carefully invert each ramekin onto a serving plate or serve the panna cotta directly in the dessert glasses.
8. Top with fresh berries or a sugar-free fruit sauce of your choice.
9. Enjoy this silky smooth Vanilla Bean Panna Cotta as an elegant and indulgent low-carb dessert.

Nutritional Information per Serving:

- Calories: 250
- Proteins: 4g
- Fats: 26g
- Carbs: 3g
- Fiber: -
- Sugar: 1g
- Sodium: 25mg
- Omega 3: 0.2g

Apple Cinnamon Crumble

Servings: 6 servings

Preparation Time: 15 minutes
Baking Time: 30-35 minutes

Ingredients:

- Apples: 4 medium-sized, peeled, cored, and thinly sliced
- Lemon juice: 1 tablespoon
- Erythritol or sweetener of choice: 2 tablespoons
- Ground cinnamon: 1 teaspoon
- Almond flour: ¾ cup (75g)
- Erythritol or sweetener of choice: ¼ cup (40g)
- Butter or coconut oil, melted: 3 tablespoons
- Chopped walnuts or pecans: ¼ cup (30g)
- Optional: Sugar-free whipped cream or low-carb vanilla ice cream for serving

Instructions:

1. Preheat the oven to 350°F (175°C) and grease a baking dish.
2. In a bowl, toss the sliced apples with lemon juice, erythritol (or sweetener of choice), and ground cinnamon until well coated. Set aside.
3. In a separate bowl, combine the almond flour, erythritol (or sweetener of choice), melted butter or coconut oil, and chopped walnuts or pecans. Mix until the ingredients are well combined and form a crumbly texture.

4. Place the coated apples in the greased baking dish and spread them evenly.
5. Sprinkle the almond flour crumble mixture over the apples, covering them completely.
6. Bake in the preheated oven for 30-35 minutes, or until the apples are tender and the crumble topping is golden brown.
7. Remove from the oven and let it cool for a few minutes before serving.
8. Serve the Apple Cinnamon Crumble warm, topped with sugar-free whipped cream or a scoop of low-carb vanilla ice cream if desired.
9. Enjoy this delicious and comforting Apple Cinnamon Crumble as a healthier twist on a classic dessert.

Nutritional Information per Serving:

- Calories: 160
- Proteins: 2g
- Fats: 13g
- Carbs: 11g
- Fiber: 4g
- Sugar: 6g
- Sodium: 5mg
- Omega 3: 0.2g

Greek Yogurt Berry Tart

Servings: 8 servings

Preparation Time: 15 minutes
Chilling Time: 2 hours

Ingredients:

For the Crust:
- Almond flour: 1 ½ cups (150g)
- Erythritol or sweetener of choice: ¼ cup (40g)
- Coconut oil, melted: 4 tablespoons
- Vanilla extract: 1 teaspoon

For the Filling:
- Greek yogurt: 2 cups (480g)
- Erythritol or sweetener of choice: ¼ cup (40g)
- Vanilla extract: 1 teaspoon

For the Topping:
- Fresh berries (strawberries, blueberries, raspberries): 2 cups (300g)
- Fresh mint leaves for garnish (optional)

Instructions:

1. In a mixing bowl, combine the almond flour, erythritol (or sweetener of choice), melted coconut oil, and vanilla extract for the crust. Mix until the ingredients are well combined and form a crumbly texture.
2. Press the mixture evenly into the bottom and sides of a tart pan or pie dish to form the crust.
3. In another bowl, mix together the Greek yogurt, erythritol (or sweetener of choice), and vanilla extract until smooth and well combined.
4. Pour the yogurt mixture into the crust and spread it evenly.
5. Arrange the fresh berries on top of the yogurt filling.
6. Optional: Garnish with fresh mint leaves for added freshness and presentation.
7. Place the tart in the refrigerator and chill for at least 2 hours to set.
8. Once chilled, slice and serve the Greek Yogurt Berry Tart as a refreshing and healthy dessert.

Nutritional Information per Serving:

- Calories: 200
- Proteins: 8g
- Fats: 15g
- Carbs: 9g
- Fiber: 3g
- Sugar: 5g
- Sodium: 40mg
- Omega 3: 9.3g

Orange Almond Cake

Servings: 8 servings

Preparation Time: 15 minutes
Baking Time: 30-35 minutes

Ingredients:

- Almond flour: 1 ½ cups (150g)
- Baking powder: 1 teaspoon
- Erythritol or sweetener of choice: ½ cup (80g)
- Salt: ¼ teaspoon
- Eggs: 4
- Fresh orange juice: ½ cup (120ml)
- Orange zest: 1 tablespoon
- Almond extract: 1 teaspoon
- Sliced almonds for topping (optional)

Instructions:

1. Preheat the oven to 350°F (175°C) and grease a round cake pan.
2. In a mixing bowl, whisk together the almond flour, baking powder, erythritol (or sweetener of choice), and salt.
3. In a separate bowl, beat the eggs until frothy. Add the fresh orange juice, orange zest, and almond extract. Mix well to combine.
4. Add the wet ingredients to the dry ingredients and stir until a smooth batter forms.
5. Pour the batter into the greased cake pan and smooth the top with a spatula.
6. Optional: Sprinkle sliced almonds on top of the batter for added texture and decoration.
7. Bake in the preheated oven for 30-35 minutes, or until the cake is golden brown and a toothpick inserted into the center comes out clean.
8. Remove from the oven and let the cake cool in the pan for a few minutes, then transfer it to a wire rack to cool completely.
9. Once cooled, slice and serve the Orange Almond Cake as a delightful and moist low-carb dessert.

Nutritional Information per Serving:

- Calories: 200
- Proteins: 8g
- Fats: 17g
- Carbs: 6g
- Fiber: 3g
- Sugar: 2g
- Sodium: 200mg
- Omega 3: 0.3g

Pistachio Rosewater Cookies

Servings: 12 cookies

Preparation Time: 15 minutes
Baking Time: 12-15 minutes

Ingredients:

- Pistachios, shelled and finely chopped: ½ cup (60g)
- Almond flour: 1 cup (100g)
- Erythritol or sweetener of choice: ¼ cup (40g)
- Rosewater: 1 tablespoon
- Butter, softened: 4 tablespoons
- Egg: 1
- Rose petals for garnish (optional)

Instructions:

1. Preheat the oven to 350°F (175°C) and line a baking sheet with parchment paper.
2. In a mixing bowl, combine the finely chopped pistachios, almond flour, erythritol (or sweetener of choice), and rosewater. Mix until well combined.
3. Add the softened butter to the mixture and mix until the butter is fully incorporated.
4. Add the egg and continue mixing until the dough comes together.
5. Roll the dough into 12 equal-sized balls and place them on the prepared baking sheet. Flatten each ball slightly with the palm of your hand.
6. Optional: Garnish each cookie with a sprinkle of rose petals for added fragrance and aesthetics.
7. Bake in the preheated oven for 12-15 minutes, or until the edges of the cookies are golden brown.

8. Remove from the oven and let the cookies cool on the baking sheet for a few minutes, then transfer them to a wire rack to cool completely.
9. Once cooled, these Pistachio Rosewater Cookies are ready to be enjoyed as a delicate and flavorful treat.

Nutritional Information per Serving (1 Cookie):

- Calories: 90
- Proteins: 3g
- Fats: 8g
- Carbs: 2g
- Fiber: 1g
- Sugar: -
- Sodium: 20mg
- Omega 3: 0.1g

Honey Roasted Figs with Greek Yogurt

Servings: 2 servings

Preparation Time: 10 minutes
Roasting Time: 10-12 minutes

Ingredients:

- Fresh figs: 4
- Honey: 2 tablespoons
- Lemon juice: 1 tablespoon
- Greek yogurt: ½ cup (120g)
- Chopped pistachios for garnish (optional)
- Fresh mint leaves for garnish (optional)

Instructions:

1. Preheat the oven to 400°F (200°C) and line a baking sheet with parchment paper.
2. Cut a small "X" on the top of each fig, about halfway down, to create an opening for the honey.
3. Place the figs on the prepared baking sheet.
4. Drizzle the honey and lemon juice over the figs, making sure to get some inside the openings.
5. Gently toss the figs to coat them evenly in the honey and lemon juice mixture.
6. Roast the figs in the preheated oven for 10-12 minutes, or until they are soft and caramelized.
7. While the figs are roasting, spoon the Greek yogurt into serving bowls.
8. Once the figs are done, remove them from the oven and let them cool for a few minutes.
9. Place the roasted figs on top of the Greek yogurt in the serving bowls.
10. Optional: Garnish with chopped pistachios and fresh mint leaves for added texture and freshness.
11. Serve the Honey Roasted Figs with Greek Yogurt as a delightful and healthy dessert or snack.

Nutritional Information per Serving:

- Calories: 150
- Proteins: 4g
- Fats: 2g
- Carbs: 32g
- Fiber: 5g
- Sugar: 27g
- Sodium: 20mg
- Omega 3: 0.2g

Yogurt and Honey Parfait with Pistachios

Servings: 2 servings

Preparation Time: 5 minutes

Ingredients:

- Greek yogurt: 1 cup (240g)
- Honey: 2 tablespoons
- Pistachios, chopped: 2 tablespoons
- Fresh berries (strawberries, blueberries, raspberries): ½ cup (75g)
- Optional: Mint leaves for garnish

Instructions:

1. In two serving glasses or bowls, layer half of the Greek yogurt in the bottom of each glass.
2. Drizzle 1 tablespoon of honey over each layer of Greek yogurt.
3. Sprinkle a tablespoon of chopped pistachios over the honey layer in each glass.
4. Add a layer of fresh berries on top of the pistachios in each glass.
5. Repeat the layers with the remaining Greek yogurt, honey, pistachios, and berries.
6. Optional: Garnish with fresh mint leaves for added freshness and presentation.
7. Serve the Yogurt and Honey Parfait with Pistachios as a delicious and nutritious dessert or breakfast option.

Nutritional Information per Serving:

- Calories: 220
- Proteins: 15g
- Fats: 8g
- Carbs: 26g
- Fiber: 3g
- Sugar: 22g
- Sodium: 50mg
- Omega 3: 0.2g

Lemon Extra Virgin Olive Oil Cake

Servings: 8 servings

Preparation Time: 15 minutes
Baking Time: 30-35 minutes

Ingredients:

- Almond flour: 1 ½ cups (150g)
- Erythritol or sweetener of choice: ½ cup (80g)
- Baking powder: 1 ½ teaspoons
- Salt: ¼ teaspoon
- Lemon zest: 2 lemons
- Eggs: 4
- Extra virgin Extra Virgin Olive Oil: ½ cup (120ml)
- Fresh lemon juice: ¼ cup (60ml)
- Greek yogurt: ½ cup (120g)
- Lemon slices for garnish (optional)

Instructions:

1. Preheat the oven to 350°F (175°C) and grease a round cake pan.
2. In a mixing bowl, whisk together the almond flour, erythritol (or sweetener of choice), baking powder, salt, and lemon zest.
3. In another bowl, beat the eggs until frothy. Add the extra virgin Extra Virgin Olive Oil, lemon juice, and Greek yogurt. Mix well to combine.
4. Add the wet ingredients to the dry ingredients and stir until a smooth batter forms.
5. Pour the batter into the greased cake pan and smooth the top with a spatula.
6. Optional: Place lemon slices on top of the batter for added visual appeal.
7. Bake in the preheated oven for 30-35 minutes, or until the cake is golden brown and a toothpick inserted into the center comes out clean.
8. Remove from the oven and let the cake cool in the pan for a few minutes, then transfer it to a wire rack to cool completely.
9. Once cooled, slice and serve the Lemon Extra Virgin Olive Oil Cake for a moist and citrusy dessert.

Nutritional Information per Serving:

- Calories: 250
- Proteins: 9g
- Fats: 20g
- Carbs: 8g
- Fiber: 3g
- Sugar: 1g
- Sodium: 180mg
- Omega 3: 0.2g

Almond Flour Baklava Bars

Servings: 12 bars

Preparation Time: 15 minutes
Baking Time: 30 minutes
Chilling Time: 1 hour

Ingredients:

For the Crust:
- Almond flour: 2 cups (200g)
- Erythritol or sweetener of choice: ¼ cup (40g)
- Salt: ¼ teaspoon
- Butter, melted: ½ cup (113g)
- Ground cinnamon: 1 teaspoon

For the Filling:
- Almonds, chopped: 1 cup (120g)
- Walnuts, chopped: 1 cup (120g)
- Ground cinnamon: 1 teaspoon
- Erythritol or sweetener of choice: ¼ cup (40g)
- Butter, melted: 4 tablespoons

For the Syrup:
- Water: ½ cup (120ml)
- Erythritol or sweetener of choice: ¼ cup (40g)
- Honey: 2 tablespoons
- Lemon juice: 1 tablespoon
- Lemon zest: 1 teaspoon

Instructions:

1. Preheat the oven to 350°F (175°C) and line a baking dish with parchment paper.
2. In a mixing bowl, combine the almond flour, erythritol (or sweetener of choice), salt, melted butter, and ground cinnamon for the crust. Mix until well combined.
3. Press the mixture evenly into the bottom of the prepared baking dish to form the crust.
4. In another bowl, mix together the chopped almonds, chopped walnuts, ground cinnamon, erythritol (or sweetener of choice), and melted butter for the filling.
5. Spread the filling evenly over the crust in the baking dish.
6. Bake in the preheated oven for 25-30 minutes, or until the edges are golden brown.
7. While the bars are baking, prepare the syrup by combining the water, erythritol (or sweetener of choice), honey, lemon juice, and lemon zest in a small saucepan. Bring the mixture to a boil, then reduce the heat and simmer for 5 minutes.
8. Remove the bars from the oven and let them cool in the baking dish for a few minutes.
9. Pour the prepared syrup over the warm bars, making sure to cover the entire surface.
10. Place the baking dish in the refrigerator and chill for at least 1 hour to allow the bars to set.
11. Once chilled, remove the bars from the baking dish and cut into individual servings.
12. Serve the Almond Flour Baklava Bars as a delectable and nutty dessert with a healthy twist.

Nutritional Information per Serving:

- Calories: 250
- Proteins: 7g
- Fats: 21g
- Carbs: 9g
- Fiber: 4g
- Sugar: 2g
- Sodium: 70mg
- Omega 3: 0.3g

Walnut Date Energy Balls

Servings: 12 energy balls

Preparation Time: 15 minutes

Ingredients:

- Walnuts: 1 cup (120g)
- Dates, pitted: 1 cup (160g)
- Unsweetened shredded coconut: ¼ cup (25g)
- Vanilla extract: 1 teaspoon
- Ground cinnamon: ½ teaspoon
- Pinch of salt
- Optional: Additional shredded coconut for rolling

Instructions:

1. In a food processor, combine the walnuts, pitted dates, shredded coconut, vanilla extract, ground cinnamon, and a pinch of salt.
2. Process the mixture until it forms a sticky dough-like consistency. If needed, you can add a teaspoon or two of water to help the ingredients bind together.
3. Once the mixture is well combined, remove it from the food processor.
4. Take about a tablespoon of the mixture and roll it into a small ball using your hands.
5. Optional: Roll the energy balls in additional shredded coconut to coat them, if desired.
6. Repeat the process with the remaining mixture, forming 12 energy balls in total.
7. Place the energy balls in an airtight container and refrigerate for at least 30 minutes to allow them to firm up.
8. Once chilled, the Walnut Date Energy Balls are ready to be enjoyed as a healthy and energizing snack.

Nutritional Information per Serving
(1 Energy Ball):

- Calories: 90
- Proteins: 2g
- Fats: 7g
- Carbs: 7g
- Fiber: 2g
- Sugar: 5g
- Sodium: -
- Omega 3: 0.3g

Coconut Yogurt Popsicles with Fresh Fruit

Servings: 6 popsicles

Preparation Time: 10 minutes
Freezing Time: 4-6 hours

Ingredients:

- Coconut milk yogurt: 2 cups (480g)
- Honey or sweetener of choice: 2 tablespoons
- Fresh mixed berries (strawberries, blueberries, raspberries): 1 cup (150g)
- Optional: Sliced kiwi or other fruits for variety

Instructions:

1. In a bowl, combine the coconut milk yogurt and honey (or sweetener of choice). Stir well to incorporate the sweetener into the yogurt.
2. Prepare your popsicle molds and arrange the fresh mixed berries evenly in each mold, leaving some space for the yogurt mixture.
3. Pour the sweetened coconut milk yogurt over the fresh fruit in the molds, filling each mold to the top.
4. Use a popsicle stick or a skewer to gently swirl the yogurt and fruit together in each mold.
5. Optional: Add additional sliced fruits like kiwi or other favorites to create a variety of flavors and colors.
6. Insert the popsicle sticks into the molds, ensuring they are centered.
7. Place the popsicle molds in the freezer and allow them to freeze for 4-6 hours, or until completely solid.
8. Once fully frozen, remove the popsicles from the molds by running warm water over the outside of the molds for a few seconds.
9. Serve the Coconut Yogurt Popsicles with Fresh Fruit as a refreshing and nutritious treat for hot days.

Nutritional Information per Serving
(1 Popsicle):

- Calories: 90
- Proteins: 1g
- Fats : 6g
- Carbs: 10g
- Fiber: 1g
- Sugar: 7g
- Sodium: 10mg
- Omega 3: 0.1g

Greek Yogurt Lemon Bars

Servings: 9 bars

Preparation Time: 15 minutes
Baking Time: 30-35 minutes
Chilling Time: 2 hours

Ingredients:

For the Crust:
- Almond flour: 1 ½ cups (150g)
- Erythritol or sweetener of choice: ¼ cup (40g)
- Salt: ¼ teaspoon
- Coconut oil, melted: ¼ cup (60ml)
- Lemon zest: 1 lemon

For the Filling:
- Greek yogurt: 1 cup (240g)
- Erythritol or sweetener of choice: ½ cup (80g)
- Lemon juice: ¼ cup (60ml)
- Lemon zest: 1 lemon
- Eggs: 2
- Almond flour: 2 tablespoons
- Baking powder: ½ teaspoon
- Optional: Powdered erythritol for dusting

Instructions:

1. Preheat the oven to 350°F (175°C) and line a square baking dish with parchment paper.
2. In a mixing bowl, combine the almond flour, erythritol (or sweetener of choice), salt, melted coconut oil, and lemon zest for the crust. Mix until well combined.
3. Press the mixture evenly into the bottom of the prepared baking dish to form the crust.

4. Bake the crust in the preheated oven for 10 minutes, then remove from the oven and set aside.
5. In another bowl, whisk together the Greek yogurt, erythritol (or sweetener of choice), lemon juice, lemon zest, eggs, almond flour, and baking powder until smooth.
6. Pour the filling mixture over the pre-baked crust in the baking dish.
7. Return the dish to the oven and bake for an additional 20-25 minutes, or until the filling is set and slightly golden on top.
8. Remove from the oven and let the lemon bars cool in the baking dish for about 10 minutes, then transfer to a wire rack to cool completely.
9. Once cooled, refrigerate the lemon bars for at least 2 hours to allow them to chill and set.
10. Before serving, dust the bars with powdered erythritol for an extra touch, if desired.
11. Cut into squares and serve the Greek Yogurt Lemon Bars as a tangy and refreshing dessert.

Nutritional Information per Serving (1 Bar):

- Calories: 170
- Proteins: 6g
- Fats: 14g
- Carbs: 6g
- Fiber: 2g
- Sugar: 2g
- Sodium: 70mg
- Omega 3: 0.2g

Desserts don't have to entail sacrificing your health and well-being. With these recipes, you may have a guilt-free sweet conclusion to your meals or a delectable snack whenever you crave something sweet. Remember, it's all about finding a happy medium and making wise decisions. You can fulfill your appetites while also feeding your health by introducing these low-carb and nutritious sweets into your diet. Experiment with the recipes in this chapter and be inventive in the kitchen. Don't be scared to explore and personalize these treats.

Happy baking and eating!

Chapter 9. Staying on Track: Tips and Strategies

Introduction:

Congratulations on your commitment to the low-carb diet! As you embark on this journey, it's important to equip yourself with the necessary tools to overcome challenges and stay motivated. Here, we're going to explore practical tips and strategies to help you navigate common hurdles, manage cravings, incorporate physical activity, and maintain your low-carb lifestyle in various social settings. Let's dive in and discover how to stay on track and achieve your goals.

1. Overcoming Common Challenges and Staying Motivated:

The low-carb diet may present challenges along the way, but with the right mindset and strategies, you can overcome them. Recognize that change takes time and focus on progress rather than perfection. Stay motivated by setting realistic and achievable goals, tracking your progress, and celebrating milestones along the way. Remind yourself of the reasons why you started this journey and the positive impact it has on your health and well-being.

2. Practical Tips for Dining Out, Social Situations, and Travel:

Eating out, attending social events, and traveling can sometimes pose challenges to your low-carb lifestyle. However, with a few simple strategies, you can stay on track. Research menus in advance, choose restaurants with low-carb options, and don't be afraid to make special requests. In social situations, focus on the company and engage in activities rather than solely on food. When traveling, pack low-carb snacks, scout local markets for fresh ingredients, and plan your meals ahead whenever possible.

3. Dealing with Cravings and Managing Hunger throughout the Day:

Cravings and hunger pangs can test your willpower, but there are effective strategies to manage them. Incorporate plenty of protein and healthy fats into your meals to promote satiety. Keep nutritious low-carb snacks on hand to curb cravings, such as nuts, seeds, and low-sugar protein bars. Drink plenty of water to stay hydrated and help control hunger. Additionally, consider incorporating intermittent fasting or mindful eating techniques to develop a healthier relationship with food.

4. Incorporating Physical Activity and Exercise into a Busy Lifestyle:

Physical activity and exercise play a crucial role in overall health and weight management. Even with a busy schedule, it's possible to incorporate movement into your daily routine. Find activities you enjoy and make them a priority. Schedule regular exercise sessions, whether it's a brisk walk, a home workout, or a fitness class. Consider incorporating strength training to build lean muscle, which can help boost metabolism and support long-term weight management.

5. *Prioritizing Self-Care and Stress Management:*

Taking care of your mental and emotional well-being is just as important as your physical health. Prioritize self-care activities that help you unwind, relax, and manage stress. Engage in activities such as meditation, yoga, deep breathing exercises, or journaling to reduce stress levels. Recognize the connection between emotions and food, and find alternative ways to cope with stress or emotional triggers that don't involve food.

6. *Building a Support Network and Accountability:*

Surrounding yourself with a supportive network can significantly impact your success. Seek like-minded individuals who share your low-carb lifestyle and connect with them through online communities, social media groups, or local meetups. Share your challenges, successes, and tips with others to provide and receive support. Consider enlisting a friend or family member as an accountability partner to keep each other motivated and on track.

Chapter 10. Conclusion

Congratulations on reaching the final chapter of this low-carb diet journey! Throughout this book, we have explored the principles of a low-carb lifestyle, delved into a variety of delicious recipes, and provided valuable tips and strategies to help you succeed. As we wrap up, let's take a moment to recap the key points, encourage you on your low-carb journey, and provide final tips for long-term success and sustainability. Remember, your health and well-being are worth prioritizing, and the choices you make today will have a positive impact on your future.

1. Recap of Key Points and Recipes:

Let's take a moment to reflect on the key points we have covered throughout this book. We started by understanding the foundations of a low-carb diet, including its benefits for weight management, blood sugar control, and overall health. We then provided a variety of delicious recipes spanning breakfast, lunch, dinner, snacks, and desserts, inspired by both US and UK cuisine and the flavors of the Mediterranean. From Cauliflower Mac and Cheese to Greek Yogurt Berry Tart, these recipes have showcased the versatility and tastiness of low-carb eating.

2. Encouragement for Your Low-Carb Journey:

Embarking on a low-carb journey can be challenging, but we want to encourage you to stay committed and motivated. Remember your reasons for starting this journey—whether it's improved health, increased energy, or a desire to make positive changes in your life. Keep in mind that every small step forward counts, and progress is a journey, not a destination. Embrace the process and celebrate your achievements along the way.

3. Final Tips for Long-Term Success and Sustainability:

To ensure long-term success with your low-carb lifestyle, it's important to adopt sustainable habits. Incorporate variety into your meals, explore new flavors and ingredients, and be open to trying different recipes. Focus on whole, unprocessed foods and prioritize nutrient-dense options. Stay mindful of portion sizes and listen to your body's hunger and fullness cues. Remember to stay hydrated, move your body regularly, and manage stress effectively. By making these practices part of your daily routine, you'll find it easier to maintain your low-carb lifestyle in the long run.

4. Inspiring You to Prioritize Your Health and Well-being:

Above all, we want to inspire you to prioritize your health and well-being. Your body is unique, and taking care of it is a lifelong journey. Embrace the power of nourishing foods, regular physical activity, and self-care practices. Believe in your ability to make positive choices that support your overall well-being.

Remember that your health is an investment that pays dividends in all aspects of your life, allowing you to live a vibrant and fulfilling life.

We hope that you feel empowered and inspired to continue your low-carb journey. We have provided you with the knowledge, recipes, and strategies to make informed choices that support your goals. Remember that this is not the end but rather the beginning of a healthier, happier you. Embrace the power of the low-carb lifestyle, listen to your body, and make choices that align with your individual needs. Prioritize your health and well-being, and enjoy the benefits that come with it.

Thank you for joining us on this low-carb adventure. May your journey be filled with delicious meals, renewed energy, and a deep sense of well-being.

Wishing you all the best on your continued success!

Appendix

WEEKLY MEAL PLANS

Please note that these following are just sample Weekly Food Plans, and you can adjust them based on your specific needs, preferences, and dietary goals. Additionally, portion sizes and specific recipes can be modified as needed to align with the desired calorie intake. Remember to listen to your body, make modifications as necessary, and consult with a healthcare professional or registered dietitian for personalized guidance.

Calorie Goal: 1800 calories per day

Day 1:
- Breakfast: Avocado and Egg Breakfast Muffins
- Snack: Greek Yogurt with Berries
- Lunch: Chicken Caesar Salad Wrap with Lettuce Wraps
- Snack: Almonds and Baby Carrots
- Dinner: Baked Salmon with Asparagus and Quinoa
- Dessert: Chia Pudding with Mixed Berries

Day 2:
- Breakfast: Veggie and Cheese Omelette
- Snack: Apple Slices with Peanut Butter
- Lunch: Mediterranean Chicken Salad with Lemon Vinaigrette
- Snack: Celery Sticks with Hummus
- Dinner: Turkey Stuffed Bell Peppers
- Dessert: Dark Chocolate Covered Strawberries

Day 3:
- Breakfast: Spinach and Mushroom Frittata
- Snack: Protein Shake with Almond Milk and Berries
- Lunch: Greek Salad with Grilled Chicken
- Snack: Hard-Boiled Eggs and Cherry Tomatoes
- Dinner: Zucchini Noodle Carbonara
- Dessert: Mixed Berry Parfait with Greek Yogurt

Day 4:
- Breakfast: Peanut Butter Banana Smoothie
- Snack: Mixed Nuts and Seeds
- Lunch: Spinach and Feta Stuffed Chicken Breast
- Snack: Cucumber Slices with Tzatziki
- Dinner: Buffalo Chicken Lettuce Wraps
- Dessert: Lemon Blueberry Cheesecake Bars

Day 5:
- Breakfast: Greek Yogurt Pancakes with Berries
- Snack: Veggie Sticks with Guacamole
- Lunch: Mediterranean Quinoa Salad with Feta
- Snack: Protein Bar or Shake
- Dinner: Baked Lemon Herb Chicken Thighs with Roasted Vegetables
- Dessert: Almond Flour Brownies

Day 6:
- Breakfast: Smoked Salmon and Cream Cheese Roll-Ups
- Snack: Trail Mix with Dried Fruit and Seeds
- Lunch: Greek Lamb Meatballs with Tzatziki Sauce
- Snack: Kale Chips
- Dinner: Beef and Broccoli Stir-Fry with Cauliflower Rice
- Dessert: Raspberry Almond Thumbprint Cookies

Day 7:
- Breakfast: Mushroom and Spinach Breakfast Casserole
- Snack: Cottage Cheese with Sliced Peaches
- Lunch: Mediterranean Tuna Salad Lettuce Wraps
- Snack: Protein Smoothie
- Dinner: Grilled Mediterranean Vegetables with Feta
- Dessert: Greek Yogurt Berry Tart

Calorie Goal: 1600 calories per day

Day 1:
- Breakfast: Veggie and Cheese Omelette
- Snack: Greek Yogurt with Berries
- Lunch: Mediterranean Chicken Salad with Lemon Vinaigrette
- Snack: Almonds and Baby Carrots
- Dinner: Grilled Salmon with Quinoa and Steamed Broccoli
- Dessert: Chia Pudding with Mixed Berries

Day 2:
- Breakfast: Spinach and Mushroom Frittata
- Snack: Apple Slices with Almond Butter
- Lunch: Greek Salad with Grilled Chicken
- Snack: Celery Sticks with Hummus
- Dinner: Turkey Stuffed Bell Peppers
- Dessert: Dark Chocolate Covered Strawberries

Day 3:
- Breakfast: Avocado and Egg Breakfast Muffins
- Snack: Protein Shake with Almond Milk and Berries
- Lunch: Quinoa and Black Bean Salad with Avocado
- Snack: Hard-Boiled Eggs and Cherry Tomatoes
- Dinner: Baked Lemon Herb Chicken Thighs with Roasted Vegetables
- Dessert: Mixed Berry Parfait with Greek Yogurt

Day 4:
- Breakfast: Peanut Butter Banana Smoothie
- Snack: Mixed Nuts and Seeds
- Lunch: Caprese Salad with Balsamic Glaze
- Snack: Cucumber Slices with Tzatziki
- Dinner: Zucchini Noodle Carbonara
- Dessert: Almond Flour Brownies

Day 5:
- Breakfast: Greek Yogurt Pancakes with Berries
- Snack: Veggie Sticks with Guacamole
- Lunch: Mediterranean Quinoa Salad with Feta
- Snack: Protein Bar or Shake
- Dinner: Spinach and Feta Stuffed Chicken Breast
- Dessert: Lemon Blueberry Cheesecake Bars

Day 6:
- Breakfast: Smoked Salmon and Cream Cheese Roll-Ups
- Snack: Trail Mix with Dried Fruit and Seeds
- Lunch: Greek Lamb Meatballs with Tzatziki Sauce
- Snack: Kale Chips
- Dinner: Buffalo Chicken Lettuce Wraps
- Dessert: Raspberry Almond Thumbprint Cookies

Day 7:
- Breakfast: Mushroom and Spinach Breakfast Casserole
- Snack: Cottage Cheese with Sliced Peaches
- Lunch: Mediterranean Tuna Salad Lettuce Wraps
- Snack: Protein Smoothie
- Dinner: Grilled Mediterranean Vegetables with Feta
- Dessert: Greek Yogurt Berry Tart

Calorie Goal: 2000 calories per day

Day 1:
- Breakfast: Scrambled Eggs with Spinach and Feta
- Lunch: Greek Chicken Salad
- Snack: Greek Yogurt Parfait
- Dinner: Baked Salmon with Lemon Dill Sauce
- Snack: Mixed Nuts

Day 2:
- Breakfast: Vegetable Frittata
- Lunch: Mediterranean Hummus Wrap
- Snack: Celery Sticks with Peanut Butter
- Dinner: Greek Lentil Salad
- Snack: Dark Chocolate Avocado Mousse

Day 3:
- Breakfast: Blueberry Almond Chia Pudding
- Lunch: Mediterranean Stuffed Pita Pockets
- Snack: Baby Carrots with Hummus
- Dinner: Grilled Steak with Asparagus and Cauliflower Mash
- Snack: Berries and Whipped Cream Parfait

Day 4:
- Breakfast: Overnight Oats
- Lunch: Greek Chickpea Salad
- Snack: Almonds
- Dinner: Roasted Chicken with Brussels Sprouts and Bacon
- Snack: Greek Yogurt with Honey and Walnuts

Day 5:
- Breakfast: Banana Nut Pancakes
- Lunch: Mediterranean Quinoa Salad
- Snack: Cucumber Slices with Hummus
- Dinner: Caprese Chicken Salad
- Snack: Apple Slices with Almond Butter

Day 6:
- Breakfast: Veggie Breakfast Casserole
- Lunch: Mediterranean Veggie Wrap
- Snack: Greek Yogurt with Berries
- Dinner: Greek Pasta Salad
- Snack: Cheese Slices

Day 7:
- Breakfast: Chia Seed Pudding with Berries
- Lunch: Turkey and Cranberry Salad Wrap
- Snack: Trail Mix
- Dinner: Prosciutto-Wrapped Asparagus with Cauliflower Mash
- Snack: Hard-Boiled Egg

Calorie Goal: 2200 calories per day

Day 1:
Breakfast: Peanut Butter Banana Smoothie
Lunch: Greek Chicken Salad
Snack: Mixed Nuts
Dinner: Baked Salmon with Lemon Dill Sauce
Snack: Greek Yogurt Parfait

Day 2:
Breakfast: Spinach and Feta Omelette
Lunch: Mediterranean Stuffed Pita Pockets
Snack: Celery Sticks with Hummus
Dinner: Greek Lentil Salad
Snack: Dark Chocolate Avocado Mousse

Day 3:
Breakfast: Blueberry Almond Chia Pudding
Lunch: Mediterranean Hummus Wrap
Snack: Almonds
Dinner: Grilled Steak with Asparagus and Cauliflower Mash
Snack: Berries and Whipped Cream Parfait

Day 4:
Breakfast: Overnight Oats
Lunch: Greek Chickpea Salad
Snack: Cheese Slices
Dinner: Roasted Chicken with Brussels Sprouts and Bacon
Snack: Greek Yogurt with Honey and Walnuts

Day 5:
Breakfast: Banana Nut Pancakes
Lunch: Mediterranean Quinoa Salad
Snack: Trail Mix
Dinner: Caprese Chicken Salad
Snack: Apple Slices with Almond Butter

Day 6:
Breakfast: Veggie Breakfast Casserole
Lunch: Mediterranean Veggie Wrap
Snack: Mixed Berries
Dinner: Greek Pasta Salad
Snack: Greek Yogurt with Berries

Day 7:
Breakfast: Chia Seed Pudding with Berries
Lunch: Turkey and Cranberry Salad Wrap
Snack: Baby Carrots with Hummus
Dinner: Prosciutto-Wrapped Asparagus with Cauliflower Mash
Snack: Hard-Boiled Egg

Customizing Your Low Carb Meal Plan

Let's explore now various strategies to customize your low carb meal plan according to your specific dietary needs, preferences, and goals. While the previous meal plans provided a starting point, it's important to tailor your meal plan to suit your individual requirements. Whether you have specific dietary restrictions, weight management goals, or health conditions, these suggestions and modifications will help you create a plan that works best for you.

1. Adapting for Dietary Restrictions:

If you have dietary restrictions or allergies, it's important to make appropriate substitutions in your meal plan. Here are a few common dietary restrictions and how to modify your low carb meal plan accordingly:

- Gluten-Free: Replace gluten-containing grains like wheat, barley, and rye with gluten-free alternatives such as quinoa, rice, or gluten-free oats.
- Dairy-Free: Substitute dairy products with non-dairy alternatives like almond milk, coconut milk, or dairy-free cheese options.
- Nut-Free: Swap nut-based ingredients with seeds or seed butter for added flavor and texture.
- Soy-Free: Use soy-free alternatives like coconut aminos instead of soy sauce or tamari.

2. Weight Management Goals:

If you have specific weight management goals, you can make adjustments to your low carb meal plan to support your objectives. Here are a few tips:

- Portion Control: Pay attention to portion sizes and practice mindful eating to avoid overeating.
- Calorie Tracking: Monitor your daily calorie intake to ensure you are in line with your weight goals.
- Incorporate More Low-Calorie Foods: Include plenty of non-starchy vegetables, lean proteins, and healthy fats in your meals to create a satisfying and balanced plate.

3. Health Conditions:

If you have certain health conditions, you may need to make additional modifications to your low carb meal plan. Here are a few examples:

- Diabetes: Monitor your carbohydrate intake and choose low glycemic index foods to help manage blood sugar levels.

- Hypertension (High Blood Pressure): Reduce sodium intake by using herbs, spices, and other flavorings to season your meals instead of salt.
- Heart Disease: Focus on heart-healthy fats like avocados, Extra Virgin Olive Oil, and fatty fish, while limiting saturated and trans fats.

4. Vegetarian or Vegan Adaptations:

If you follow a vegetarian or vegan lifestyle, you can customize your low carb meal plan accordingly. Here are a few suggestions:

- Plant-Based Proteins: Include protein-rich plant foods like tofu, tempeh, legumes, and quinoa as alternatives to animal-based proteins.
- Abundant Veggies: Fill your plate with a variety of non-starchy vegetables for fiber, vitamins, and minerals.
- Healthy Fats: Incorporate plant-based fats from sources like avocados, nuts, seeds, and Extra Virgin Olive Oil.

5. Cultural and Culinary Preferences:

Embrace the diversity of flavors and culinary traditions by customizing your low carb meal plan to suit your cultural preferences. Consider the following:

- Ethnic Cuisine: Explore low carb recipes inspired by various cuisines, such as Mexican, Indian, Thai, or Middle Eastern, and adapt them to fit your dietary needs.
- Traditional Dishes: Modify traditional family recipes by swapping high carb ingredients with low carb alternatives while preserving the flavors and essence of the dish.

Final Considerations:

Creating a personalized and adaptable low carb meal plan is key to long-term success and sustainability. By understanding your specific dietary needs, goals, and preferences, you can make adjustments to the sample meal plans provided and create a plan that works best for you.

Remember, nutrition is a journey, and it's important to listen to your body, experiment with different foods, and seek guidance from healthcare professionals or registered dietitians for personalized advice and support.

By customizing your low carb meal plan, you can embark on a journey towards better health, nourishment, and enjoyment of delicious meals while staying true to your individual needs and preferences. Prioritize your well-being and make conscious choices that align with your unique circumstances.

Mindful Eating: Nourishing Your Body and Mind

Mindful eating is a practice that encourages us to develop a deeper awareness and appreciation of the food we consume. In today's fast-paced world, we often find ourselves eating on the go, distracted by screens, and rushing through meals. Mindful eating offers a different approach—one that brings our attention back to the present moment and cultivates a greater connection with our food.

At its core, mindful eating is about paying attention to the sensory experiences of eating—savoring the flavors, textures, and aromas. It involves engaging all our senses and fully immersing ourselves in the act of eating. By doing so, we can cultivate a healthier relationship with food and develop a more intuitive understanding of our body's needs.

One key aspect of mindful eating is slowing down. Taking the time to eat without rushing allows us to tune in to our body's hunger and fullness cues. It gives us the opportunity to savor each bite and notice the subtle changes in our appetite as we eat. By being present in the moment, we can better recognize when we are truly satisfied and prevent overeating.

Mindful eating also involves cultivating non-judgmental awareness of our thoughts, emotions, and sensations that arise during eating. It encourages us to observe any tendencies towards emotional or mindless eating without judgment. Through this awareness, we can begin to differentiate between true physical hunger and other triggers that may lead to unnecessary eating.

Practicing mindful eating can have numerous benefits for our overall well-being. It can help improve digestion by promoting slower and more thorough chewing, aiding in the breakdown of food. It can also enhance the enjoyment and satisfaction we derive from our meals, leading to a greater sense of fulfillment and contentment.

Moreover, mindful eating can contribute to a healthier relationship with food. It can reduce feelings of guilt or shame associated with eating, as it encourages self-compassion and acceptance. By reconnecting with the body's natural cues, we can better nourish ourselves in a way that supports our individual needs and preferences.

Incorporating mindful eating into our daily lives may take practice and patience. It requires creating space for meals, minimizing distractions, and approaching eating with curiosity and openness. Over time, the practice of mindful eating can become a valuable tool for self-care, self-awareness, and overall holistic well-being.

Remember, mindful eating is not about rigid rules or restrictions—it's about developing a compassionate and attuned relationship with food. By bringing mindfulness to our meals, we can transform eating into a nourishing and joyful experience that nurtures both our body and mind.

Unlocking Your Journey to Success: Embracing the Power of Mindset

Embarking on a low-carb (or any other diet) lifestyle requires more than just dietary changes. It demands a shift in mindset, a deep-rooted commitment, and unwavering perseverance. In this section, we delve into the transformative power of mindset and share inspiring stories of individuals who have achieved long-term success with a low-carb lifestyle. Get ready to unlock your true potential and pave the way for lasting positive change.

Discover Your Why - Your journey begins with uncovering your personal "why." Meet Sarah, a woman who struggled with her weight for years. She had tried numerous diets but always found herself reverting to old habits. Determined to make a change, she embarked on a low-carb lifestyle, but this time with a clear purpose: to become the healthiest version of herself for her children. Sarah's story serves as a powerful reminder that finding your why provides the fuel to stay committed and overcome any obstacle that comes your way. Through reflective exercises and practical tips, we guide you in discovering your own motivation and creating a strong sense of purpose.

Building Resilience - Meet John, a remarkable individual who not only achieved incredible physical transformation but also developed an unwavering mindset that propelled him towards long-term success with a low-carb lifestyle. John's journey began like many others, filled with doubts, setbacks, and moments of frustration. However, what set him apart was his ability to cultivate resilience and harness the power of his mindset.

John recognized that mindset played a pivotal role in his journey. He understood that to achieve lasting change, he needed to shift his perspective and adopt a growth mindset. He embraced the belief that challenges were opportunities for growth and that setbacks were not roadblocks but stepping stones on his path to success.

To cultivate this resilient mindset, John implemented several strategies. He developed a strong support system of like-minded individuals who shared his goals and aspirations. They became his cheerleaders, providing encouragement, accountability, and a safe space to share his challenges and triumphs. John attended support groups and sought guidance from professionals who specialized in mindset coaching.

John also understood the importance of self-compassion and self-care. He practiced mindfulness techniques, such as meditation and gratitude, to cultivate a positive mindset. When faced with cravings or moments of temptation, he reminded himself of his "why" and tapped into his deep sense of purpose. He learned to listen to his body's signals, recognizing the difference between emotional hunger and true physical hunger.

In times of adversity, John viewed setbacks as learning opportunities. Instead of berating himself for a slip-up, he examined what triggered it and used it as a chance to reflect, learn, and make adjustments moving forward. He celebrated his successes, no matter how small, and embraced a mindset of progress rather than perfection.

John also incorporated physical activity into his daily routine, recognizing the profound impact it had on his mindset. Exercise became his outlet for stress relief, a way to boost his mood, and a source of empowerment. He discovered that movement not only transformed his body but also nurtured his mental well-being.

Through these practices, John built resilience and an unyielding belief in his ability to achieve his goals. He embraced the challenges that came his way, viewing them as opportunities for growth and self-discovery. His mindset became his strongest ally, propelling him forward even in the face of obstacles.

By sharing John's inspiring journey, we want to encourage you to develop your own resilient mindset. These are practical strategies and insights to help cultivate resilience, overcome setbacks, and embrace a growth mindset. Remember, building resilience is a lifelong process, but with dedication, determination, and the right mindset, you can overcome any challenge and achieve lasting success on your low-carb journey.

Creating Lasting Habits - Let's meet Emma, a beacon of strength and self-love who discovered the transformative power of a low-carb lifestyle. Emma's journey was not just about weight loss; it was a profound exploration of self-acceptance, empowerment, and embracing her true worth.

She had struggled with her weight and body image for years, battling negative self-talk and societal pressures. However, when she embarked on her low-carb journey, something shifted within her. She made a conscious decision to prioritize self-love and embrace her body for all that it was capable of.

To embark on this transformation, Emma knew she needed to reframe her mindset. She challenged the limiting beliefs that had held her back for so long and replaced them with empowering thoughts. Instead of focusing on what her body lacked, she celebrated its strength, resilience, and beauty.

One of the key aspects of Emma's journey was developing a positive relationship with food. She no longer saw food as the enemy but rather as nourishment and a source of

joy. Emma learned to listen to her body's cues and make mindful choices that honored her well-being. She indulged in nutritious meals without guilt and savored the experience of eating mindfully.

In her quest for self-love and empowerment, Emma also surrounded herself with positive influences. She sought out supportive communities, whether online or in-person, where she could connect with others who shared her values and aspirations. These connections provided inspiration, motivation, and a sense of belonging.

Emma also embraced self-care practices that nourished her mind, body, and soul. She prioritized activities that brought her joy, such as practicing yoga, journaling, and spending time in nature. These self-care rituals allowed her to recharge, find balance, and cultivate a deep sense of self-worth.

Through her journey, she discovered the incredible power of self-love and self-acceptance. She let go of unrealistic expectations and comparisons and embraced her unique journey. Emma recognized that her worth was not determined by a number on a scale but by the love and respect she had for herself.

Remember that your journey is unique. You possess the power to embrace a mindset that fuels your progress and leads to long-term success. The stories shared here, along with the insights and strategies provided, serve as beacons of inspiration. Commit to your goals, trust in your capabilities, and never underestimate the transformative power of mindset. You have the ability to unlock your journey to success and create a life of health, vitality, and joy.

CONVERSION TABLES

U.S. Measurement	Metric Measurement
teaspoon (tsp)	5 milliliters (mL)
tablespoon (tbsp)	15 milliliters (mL)
fluid ounce (fl oz)	30 milliliters (mL)
cup	240 milliliters (mL)
pint (pt)	480 milliliters (mL)
quart (qt)	960 milliliters (mL)
gallon (gal)	3.8 liters (L)
ounce (oz)	28 grams (g)
pound (lb)	453 grams (g)
inch (in)	2.54 centimeters (cm)
foot (ft)	30.48 centimeters (cm)

Fahrenheit (°F)	Celsius (°C)
225°F	107°C
250°F	121°C
275°F	135°C
300°F	149°C
325°F	163°C
350°F	177°C
375°F	191°C
400°F	204°C
425°F	218°C
450°F	232°C
475°F	246°C
500°F	260°C

Bonus

Thanks for Buying this Book!
Download your 250 Pages FREE and Exclusive
"Low-Carb Companion"
Use the QR Code below.

Please also remember to leave a Review on Amazon!
You will help other people make their choice.